INTO

THE

CANCER

WOODS

With Jesus, Friends and Scripture

Terry Wolfe

DEDICATION

For my son Jason, his wife Tara and daughter Emerson for being my North Star and making sure my foundation was laid on a rock. Luke 6:48

And to my prayer warriors - you stood in the gap for eight months with your prayers and encouragement. You are James 5:16

Love you all to the moon and back!

SPECIAL THANKS

To Carl Nelson, pastor at Village 7 Presbyterian Church and head of Pastoral Care. He was faithful in seeing me at EVERY chemotherapy session. We laughed, shared God's Word. He encouraged not only me but the nurses and other patients. He is a true man of God.

To the pastors and elders at Village 7 Presbyterian for their faithful prayer cards that I received every Wednesday from the beginning to the end of the journey. They meant more than you will ever know. Thank you.

To the nurses in the Chemo Lab at Memorial Hospital Central. Their calling from God is clear and their reward will be great in heaven.

To my editor Barry Hickey. In writing, red ink is good. It adds or eliminates what is needed in the story line. Red ink corrects grammar and phrases to make the story flow. Red ink does wonderful things.

PHOTOGRAPHS

Cover photograph by Terry Wolfe

Photograph of Terry Wolfe & Pop Pop by Julie Justus

Back cover photograph of Terry Wolfe and Annie by Aaron Winter

ISBN-13: 978-1484093320

With my horse Pop Pop

PREFACE

I was born in El Dorado, Kansas in 1946. My dad had just gotten out of the Navy. That same year my maternal grandparents (the Wilsons) bought a ranch two miles north of the spectacular Garden of the Gods on the northwest side of Colorado Springs, Colorado. It was a beautiful area cradled in the foothills of Pikes Peak.

Two years later, my parents and I joined them. My dad helped my grandparents in their cattle and registered Quarter Horse business. My mom was a "stay at home" mom.

In 1953 my parents started the Flying W Ranch on the property, offering chuckwagon suppers two nights a week during the summer months on what was known as the South Douglas Pasture. Besides boarding horses for local horse lovers, we started renting out horses for daily rides in the foothills. I was a part of the business from the beginning. People could ride a horse to the chuckwagon dinner area and meet family and friends for dinner before riding back to the barns after the show.

We might have had twenty people a night when we started, but by 2012 we had a thousand visitors daily, seven days a week, during our long season. People weren't renting horses anymore; they came from around the world to see our fabulous outdoor western stage shows under the stars and to enjoy our chuckwagon grub as a reminder of The Old West.

I did take a break from the ranch in the early 70's. I went to college and got an elementary teaching degree. I taught at an elementary school in Denver for four years.

I returned to Colorado Springs, taught as a substitute teacher for awhile and got involved with the family business once again as the buyer for our ten retail shops. One was a Christian book store. I worked with our Flying W Ranch employees on many levels. During the slower winter months we offered an indoor show inside our comfortable steak house.

The Flying W Ranch was a year-round thriving business for sixty years. It would still be open but nature had its way with the cataclysmic Waldo Canyon Fire on June 26, 2012. Along with hundreds of nearby homes, the entire Flying W Ranch was burned to the ground. But that's another story...

I have treasured memories of the ranch; with bears, deer, rattlesnakes and skunks roaming the eating area. I also greeted busloads of anxious camera-toting tourists eager for an adventure.

I married one of our entertainers in 1972. We divorced in 1977. I have a great son, Jason, born in 1975. He is a lawyer living in Windsor, Colorado with his wonderful wife Tara and daughter Emerson.

I became a Christian during the divorce. I have led and been involved in many Women's Bible studies over the years. At the present time I am a member of Village 7 Presbyterian, part of the Presbyterian Church in America.

To think the Living God, the Creator of the universe died for me and wants a relationship with me... doesn't get any better than that.

I love the arts. I do black and white photography and have been in two galleries in Colorado Springs. I do wheel throwing pottery (great for the mental outlook). I am trying to write a children's book. I love to ride my horse Pop Pop. She was born on the 4th of July. I also love walking my dog Annie, a Border Collie/Lab mix that I got from the National Mill Dog Rescue. Gourmet cooking is a love I got from my mom. I love to have friends and family over for dinner. They are always willing to try something! There is nothing like curling up with a new cooking magazine or cookbook.

I have lived in Colorado Springs all my life... same house for thirty-eight years (shocking), have had bears, deer, raccoons and a mountain lion in my yard. Ah, life on the West Side of the now sprawling city known as Colorado Springs.

I pray you may find encouragement from what you are about to read.

Terry Wolfe

CHAPTER 1 - JULY

MY LIFE BEFORE CANCER

I was diagnosed with invasive ductal carcinoma in July of 2011. Breast Cancer. I was 64 years old.

Some of my friends had Cancer in the past. My heart went out to them but I have to admit, I took Cancer for granted. It was a disease that affected people throughout my life. Friends and family died from all sorts of other diseases: diabetes, strokes, heart attacks, old age... Over 180,000 American women are diagnosed annually. Breast Cancer was something I paid too little attention to until it was mine to own... And own it I did...

It occurred at some point that I should write a book based on these emails, prayer journey notes, and return emails to encourage others. The books on Cancer I have read are not like this.

I saw Cancer as a journey or road trip with Jesus. It was like I was walking along doing well and He said, "Excuse me. I think I want to walk with you on the road called Cancer for awhile. Trust me for the end result."

The arc of my story follows both the course of my treatment, its effects and challenges and my walk and growth with the Lord. I am Cancer free after eight months of chemotherapy and a full right-side mastectomy. No radiation was needed. The surgery was February 3, 2012.

AND THE FATHER WILL DANCE
(A wonderful musical arrangement by Mark Hayes that I listened to with the following lyrics:

"And the Father will dance over you in joy!
He will take delight in whom he loves.
Is that a choir I hear singing the praises of God?
No, the Lord God himself is exulting o'er you in song!
And he will joy over you in song!
My soul will make it boast in God,
for he has answered all my cries,
his faithfulness tome is sure as the dawn of a new day
Awake my soul and sing!
Let my spirit rejoice in God!
Sing O daughter of Zion, with all of your heart!
Cast away fear, for you have been restored!
Put on the garment of praise as on a festival day.
Join with the Father in glorious, jubilant song." (Based on Zephaniah 3:14, 17. Psalm 34: 2, 4.)

"I am with you, I am with you, I am with you. Heaven's bells continually peal with the promise of My Presence... My desire is that My sheep hear My voice continually, for I am the ever-present Shepherd." (From Jesus Calling. Jeremiah 29:12-13; John 10:14, page 317)

"And they follow me." (John 10:27)

"We should follow our Lord as unhesitatingly as sheep follow their shepherd. He has the right to lead us wherever He pleases. We are not our own, we are brought with a price... Wherever Jesus may lead us, He goes before us. If we don't know where we are going, we know with whom we go. With such a companion, who will dread the perils of the

road?" (From Morning and Evening by Charles H. Spurgeon, page 525)

THE CANCER JOURNEY

The Lord gave me these words when I was standing in my backyard seeking guidance. I knew whether I lived or died it would be okay.

"Do not be afraid for I am with you. Do not anxiously look about you, for I am your God. I will strengthen you. Surely I will help you. Surely I will uphold you with my righteous right hand." (Isaiah 41:10)

"And The Lord is the one who goes ahead of you; He will be with you. He will not fail you or forsake you. Do not fear, or be dismayed." (Deuteronomy 31:8)

I had a mammogram on July 20, 2011. The nurse asked what the very large lump was on the top of my right breast. I said I had no idea, never thinking it was Cancer. She was shocked at my relaxed attitude and was very concerned. She said I needed a biopsy immediately. One was scheduled July 23, 2011.

The first biopsy was negative. I had the results sent to Dr. Larry Dillon. He called had said that due to the size of the mass he was asking for another one. That one came back positive. He suggested Dr. Paulishak for surgery, Dr Hoyer for oncology and Dr. Ridings for radiation. I was in shock. The next two weeks I had appointments and tests every day, sometimes twice a day. It was recommended that I have chemotherapy, then surgery, then radiation. All would be done by the end of March. From the beginning I did everything my doctors told me to do.

I asked my son Jason his family and my sister Leigh Ann and her family for prayer. I then slowly started to tell friends and co-workers who put me on their various churches' prayer chains. To keep everyone updated I sent out weekly emails with updates, prayer requests and quotes from scripture to encourage them and me.

This book is a collection of emails, notes From my Prayer Journal, and my personal truth cards (index cards I carry with biblical scripture, sermons and devotionals I use for encouragement and to remind me of truths).

I also recorded my personal goals so that friends, family, patients in the chemo lab, and the medical staffs I encountered would see Jesus in me, be encouraged, and attend church every Sunday.

CHAPTER 2 – AUGUST

Email outbox August 2nd

One of Pastor Mark Bates sermons at (Village 7, a Presbyterian Church.

A teaching titled, *"God is in the Details"*.

"'You may not always understand but you can always trust God's work of providence, one of His most holy, wise, and powerful, preserving and governing all his creation and their actions.' (Westminster Short Catechism question II) *He closed his teaching with, 'are not two sparrows sold for a cent? And yet not one of them will fall to the ground apart from your Father. But the very hairs of your head are all numbered.'"*

"Therefore do not fear; you are of more value than many sparrows." (Matthew 10:29-30)

Closing thought:

I thought God knows soon I will have no hair and yet He knows each hair that will be coming back and when!

Email outbox: August 3rd

Good Evening:

I love the rain, windows are open. My dog Annie is sleeping on the couch. Ahhh, life is good. I talked to Dr. Paulishak's office today. She is seeing me Tuesday instead of this Thursday to study the results of all the tests I will be taking tomorrow and Thursday.

I asked her (whomever called me), after she said they wanted to make sure they knew what I and they were "up against," if there was prayerful hope (as there is no such thing as luck). I might not have to go through chemo. She did her broad strokes to protect herself but I got the idea there is prayerful hope, maybe.

I prayed off and on today that, *"You LORD can and could heal me with a touch, a thought like the woman with the issue of blood who touched the hem of His robe. (Matthew 9:20).*

God can heal me through doctors, and chemo, surgery, and radiation. I asked Him if at all possible that I wouldn't have to go through chemo, but, if that is His will for me then ok let me do it with grace and dignity and be a worthy witness to Him. But I know me... I throw my Bible on the shelf and shake my fist at God asking why??? But there is hope.

"For my Thoughts are not your Thoughts, neither are your ways My ways, declares The Lord." (Isaiah 55:8)

What a journey I have started! Thank you all for your prayers. God is doing a mighty work for His glory. I hope I don't blow it. Tomorrow I have an ultrasound at 7am; a biopsy after that and then a lovely ET scan.

Email outbox: August 3rd

Good Evening:

Tomorrow my day is as follows:
8:30: MRI and chest x-ray
12:30: Echo scan
2:30: Dr. Ridings - Radiology (first time to talk to her).
3:30: Sherry, Dr. Hoyer's nurse. Up to two hours to tell me everything I could or would want to know about chemo (lovely).

Thank you for your prayers, smiles and just being you. After six months of chemo I expect I will be back to my old feisty self. As I walked around the village (our Flying W Ranch stores) since I have known I have Cancer and the doctors have said it is curable, I realize how others have it far worse than me. I have noticed wheelchairs where people are in them for life; children with huge problems from downs syndrome to braces. This is a season in my life, one more thing on the plate. I will be stronger, wiser, and closer to God for it all. There is a saying, *"The eagles that fly in the high air currents don't worry how they will cross the rivers."* I like that.

Email outbox: August 4th

Good Evening:

My, what a long day!!! When I met with Dr. Ridings some of the results were in from the testing that had been done. The PET scan and biopsy of the lymph node confirm the need for chemo. The lymph node is negative they think (don't you love it) and behind the mass where the Cancer is, it is dark (a good sign). I am a stage 2 but the grade (I think that is the word) is 3. It is aggressive, thus chemo is needed. I have a stack of prescriptions to get filled... all for nausea.

Dr. Hoyer rescheduled at the last minute so I will see him sometime on Monday. Thank you all for your prayers and VERY encouraging emails. I am going to look at wigs tomorrow with my sister Leigh Ann and then take her to Denver International airport. I was tired and overwhelmed from the tests and talks with the doctors. So much to hear and learn. When it is quiet I recite my praise songs and hymns. I could feel your prayers.

Closing thought:
"...And Jesus lifted up his eyes and said; "Father, I thank Thee that Thou has heardest me." (John 11:41)

"This is very strange and unusual order. Lazarus is still in the grave and the thanksgiving precedes the miracle of resurrection... The song of victory is sung before the battle

has been fought. Praise is really the most vital repertory ministry to the working of the miracles. Miracles are wrought by spiritual power. Spiritual power is always proportioned to our faith. Nothing so pleases God in connection with our prayers and our praise and nothing so blesses the man who prays as the praise which he offers." (From Streams in the Desert, page 233)

Email outbox: August 5th

Good Morning:

This morning I read a meditation from C.H. Spurgeon's Morning and Evening. I found a sentence that made my spirit leap with joy.

"We know that in all things God works for the good of those who love Him." (Romans 8:28)

"The Christian doesn't merely hold this as a theory, but he knows the poisonous drugs mixed in fit proportions have worked the cure." (Page 436)

Email inbox: Thoughts from Pastor Scott Vaughn

It never ceases to amaze me when God uses great voices of the Saints in the past to speak such healing into our lives today! Thank you Lord! Our thoughts and prayers continue to be with you.

Email inbox: Jan Allums

I look forward to your messages! You are able to see God work firsthand and are a testimony to all of us!

Email outbox: August 6th

Good Evening:

What a fun day I had with my sister! Leigh Ann and I went to a place a friend told me about in Denver (Linda's Boutique), owned by a woman named Mary. I purchased two great wigs and some hats. One is a full wig and the other is called "hat hair". I need my ball caps! (Will I ever grow up?) The color is like mine and the cut is very close. My full wig has bangs! Shocking to me.

Leigh Ann picked it out. I like it. I will be going up to Denver sometime next week for a fitting and Mary will cut it. She gave me great advice: cut my hair with scissors VERY close to the scalp and not a "buzz" cut as it would be hard to sleep on or feel funny as I am not used to that kind of a cut. She said my hair will not come out all at once. One of her friends, when the hair started to fall out, decided to climb on her Harley Davidson motorcycle and let the wind do the rest. I could jump on my own firecracker, my horse Pop Pop and do the same... I feel for the first time I have control and I laugh with meaning.

Closing thought:

"But as for me, I shall sing of Thy strength; Yes, I shall joyfully sing of Thy loving kindness in the morning, for Thou hast been my stronghold and a refuge in the day of my distress." (Psalm 59:16)

Email outbox: August 7th

Good Afternoon:

Some of you already know that I have been diagnosed with Breast Cancer. It is stage 2, class 3 on the right side. I start chemo soon. They will put a drainage port in me on the left side. I would covet your prayers for the next seven months. After chemo they will operate to get what is left out and then six weeks of radiation. The first phase of chemo is every fourteen days (four visits over two months). Then there is a break of three weeks followed by the second phase. Four visits every three weeks over a twelve week course.

I am standing on:

"Do not fear for I am with you, do not anxiously look about you, for I am your God, I will strengthen you surly I will help you, Surely I will uphold you with My Righteous right hand." Isaiah 41:10

I have started emailing family and friends including the teachers with what is happening daily between tests and meeting doctors. (The teachers are a circle of prayer group friends and seasonal coworkers from the Flying W Ranch working in the Chuckwagon retail shops and at the front gate when schools aren't in session.) I will add you so more friends and trusted employees can know what to pray for and when. I am going to use these emails as a journal and at the end, maybe a book? Thinking out loud... I have great peace and quiet... prayer works. But then I haven't had my first chemo injection yet. I do know that God knew from the foundations of the world that today I would be dealing with this.

And Romans 8:28 all is all....

Email inbox: Thoughts from Jan Allums:

I'm so glad Leigh Ann was still here and you could experience this together. What amazing things God is doing! Who would have ever dreamed?

"Blessed is the man who makes the Lord his trust." (Psalm 40:4)

Email Outbox: August 8th

To Deena Stuart:

I have a peace and joy I have never known every morning. The Lord gives such encouragement during my quiet time. I hate to say it, but I am looking forward to what will be happening next. (Is this sick? or the Lord?)

My Prayer Journal
August 8th

Dear Lord... Abba Father,

I pray I will be a good witness for you during this season of my life. That I will focus on your Word (truth), that I will dwell on Phil. 4:8, *"To dwell on beauty."* I ask the side effects to be livable (small). Your grace IS sufficient. I thank you in advance that at the end of this thorny road it will be a joyful end. Encourage Jason, Tara, Leigh Ann and Ruth. Find them verses to stand on. Thank you to all who are praying for me.

Email outbox: August 8th

Good Evening:

Tomorrow I have a CAT scan at 11:00 and Tuesday I see Dr. Paulishak at 9 and Dr. Hoyer at 10:15. I will then know when the port and the chemo will start. Thank you for your words of encouragement.

Today in church during the offering, the words of the first stanza of "Be Still, My Soul" were on the screen, just the piano was playing. I wrote the words down:

"Be still my soul; The Lord is on thy side, bear patiently the cross of grief or pain; Leave to thy God to order and provide; In every change the faithful will remain. Be still, my soul; the best thy heavenly Friend through thorny ways lead to a joyful end."(Katharina Amalia Dorothea Von Schlegel. 1697-1768, translated by Jane Borthwick)

There is hope!

Email inbox: from Bonnie McGowan:

I thought of you a lot today. I wondered how I would be if I heard, "Cancer for me". All I can do is look back and remember how He carried me through life's tribulations. He never left me down or forsook me, just one step at a time is all He asks you to take.

Email inbox: from my son Jason:

I found Invasive Ductal Carcinoma... here is what the Komen Foundation website has on it; "Cancer that has spread from the original location (milk ducts or lobules) into the surrounding breast tissue and possibly into the lymph nodes and other parts of the body. Invasive ductal carcinoma begins in the milk ducts. Invasive lobular Cancer begins in the lobules of the breast.

I wrote back:

Thanks. It doesn't sound good, does it?

He wrote back:

No it doesn't but based on what else you've told me it certainly could be worse. You've caught it early, you are treating it aggressively and I know you'll come out the other side. There are several short prayers in the Book of Common Prayer. One of which I thought I'd share with you as you begin this journey....

"O God, the source of all health: So fill my heart with faith in your love, that with calm expectancy I may make room for your power to possess me and gracefully accept your healing through Jesus Christ our Lord. Amen."

I have found lately, that one prayer that I can commit to memory and recite when I need it can help me though a tough moment. Just a few quick seconds bring me back to center...

I love you and I pray for you continually.

Email outbox: August 10th

Good Evening:

I am sending this to people I work with and dear family members. To get everyone at once up to speed on this journey The Lord has placed me on. An email to all will be easier than different groups.

Today I saw Dr Paulishak (breast surgeon) and Dr Hoyer (oncologist) at separate times and places. They told me the following: The Cancer is moving in the right breast and so I don't have the choice of just having a lumpectomy. I will have to have a mastectomy after the chemo. I will have the first phase of chemo every fourteen days for four times (Two months more or less), then three weeks off. The Phase 2 of chemo (a different drug) will be every three weeks for four times, then three weeks off. Next is surgery, then three weeks off followed by radiation.

After several months off chemo the side effects should be gone. I also had more blood work at Dr. Hoyer's office to see if it might be necessary to have both breasts removed at time of surgery.

Monday the 15th all morning from 7am to 12:30 PM they will do a centennial node biopsy and put the port in. Friday the 19th, I will have my first chemo. Whatever the side effects are will be the same all four times. So for the prayer requests; the side effects will be minimal but specifically that the fatigue won't be bad and my blood will stay healthy and normal to fight off infections (due to my thin skin and heredity I bruise and bleed easily).

I hope that I will be a good witness for the Lord. That people will see Jesus in me and not some old woman nagging about having Cancer. I want to be digging wells as I go on this journey as in *Psalm 84:5-6; "Blessed is the man whose strength is in Thee, who passing through the Valley of Baca, make it a well."*(paraphrased)

There is a praise song that has the following line in it. "God is good all the time. All the time God is good."

I know he is allowing this for His glory and my good. "*All is all,*" in Romans 8:28 and His ways and thoughts aren't ours. I have peace and trust in the Great I Am. He is Jehovah-Rapha (the God who heals) I believe He will heal me. He is also Jehovah-jireh (the Lord will provide) and Jehovah- Raah (the Lord my Shepherd) to name a few of His names.

Closing thought:

"O God the source of all health: So fill my heart with faith in your love, that with calm expectancy I may make room for your power to posses me, and gracefully accept your healing through Jesus Christ our Lord. Amen" (From the Book of Common Prayer)

Thank you all for standing in the gap for me at this time. James 5:16 is true!

Email inbox: from Jason:

That was a very eloquent way of putting your situation out there. I'll see you tomorrow night. We are praying for you.

I wrote back:

Knowing you are there praying is so important to me! To have a son who prays is more important than tons of people who want to help out. I love you! See you tomorrow night. Drive safe. Love you more than words can say – mom.

Email inbox: from Jan Allums:

Thank you for allowing us to go through this hard time with you. We are honored to be called prayer warriors in this and to watch God's mighty power!

I wrote back:

Thank you... It is a journey and I am really excited to see what God will do in all our lives.

Email inbox: from Zetta Henson

Hi Terry:

We just wanted you to know that we are praying for you and thinking of you al the time. You were such encouragement to us last year and we want to return the favor in any way that we can. Please let us know if there is ANYTHING, and we mean ANYTHING, that we can do for you.

We love you,
Jayson and Zetta.

Email outbox: August 10th

Hi Jayson and Zetta:

Thank you. Prayers are what I want and need. I really am doing well. God is in control. I sense something really amazing is going on as I walk this road before me. I have a peace and contentment that has to be from the Lord. I really smile and laugh. But I do have my times of tears, usually alone and not for long.

James 5:16 is true.

T.

Email outbox: August 11th

Good Morning:

I want all of you to know that I am praying God will bless you beyond your wildest dreams because you are praying for me. That God will meet all your needs through Christ and these next few months will be spring to you as it will be for me. This morning in my quiet time I read the following:

"See! The winter is past; the rains are over and gone. Flowers appear on the earth; The season of singing has come, the cooing of doves is heard in our land." (Song of Solomon 2:11-12)

"As sure as winter came, it will eventually leave. The same holds true for the winter of the soul. One day God will surprise you with the sight and song of spring... in the darkest winter God can surprise you with spring." (The Hungry Heart by Jan Carlberg, page 141)

Isn't that exciting?????

T.

Email inbox: from Deena Stuart:

I hear the joy and thank the Lord for His presence with you. We're praying God's BEST for you.

Email inbox: from Bob Stuart:

Deena and I love you dearly. In our devotional time we lift you before the Lord, asking that he envelope you with his love and grant you peace that strengthens you in your walk.

"May he be your lamp that lightens your darkness (2 Sam. 22:29) and your comfort that goes beyond understanding."

In our Spurgeon devotional today, the great preacher said, *"Am I in the dark? Then thou, O Lord, wilt lighten my darkness. Before long things will change. Affairs may grow more and more dreary, and cloud may be piled upon cloud; but if it grows so dark that I cannot see my own hand, still I will see the hand of the Lord."* He is light at the end of the tunnel, the One who promises to be with us when we walk through our dark valleys and to bring us safely to the other side.

Truth card:

"If the clouds be full of rain, they empty themselves upon the earth." (Ecclesiastes. 11:3)

"How can we have rain without clouds? Our troubles have always brought us blessings and they always will. They are dark chariots of bright grace...our God may drench us with grief, but He will refresh us with mercy. Our Lord's love letters often come to us in black-edged envelopes." (From Springs in the Desert, page 242)

Truth card:

"There couldst have no power at all against me except it were given thee from above." (John 19:11)

"Nothing that is not God's will can come into the life of one who trusts and obeys God." (From Streams in the Desert, page 243)

Truth card:

"Be silent unto God and let Him mold thee." (Psalm 46:10)

"Rest pauses contribute to the finer music of life." (From Springs in the Valley, page 242)

Email outbox: August 14th

Thank you all for your prayers. Just a reminder - tomorrow I begin this journey for real. At 7am will have a lymph node biopsy. Pray no Cancer is found that it is still only in the right breast. At 10am they will put me under and the port will go in, about ninety minutes and then recovery time. Home around 1:30. Pray all goes well and there are no complications.

Email inbox: from Pastor Scott Vaughn:

I am praying for you this morning. I pray God's grace, peace, and sufficiency over you. I pray He will pour his clarity and discernment through your doctors and that it would be His healing grace that is ministered through them.

And I boldly pray for His favor upon you and for you to be intimately and powerfully aware of His presence.

In and through the morning:

Email inbox: from Deena Stuart:

"When we shoot an arrow, we look to the fall of it; when we send a ship to sea, we look for the return of it; and when we sow seed, we look for the harvest; and so when we sow our prayers into God's bosom, shall we not look for an answer?" (Richard Sibbes)

Prayer Journal
August 14th

I am thankful that nothing is not God's will come into my life because I am trusting and obeying God. I am His child and He wants the very best for me. Tomorrow it all begins. Lord, I ask you will guide the doctor's hands, my body will accept the port and I can go to work to check up and maybe walk Chloe. (Chloe is our adorable miniature donkey that I would walk around the village at the Flying W. Everyone from bikers to toddlers wanted to pose for a picture with her.) I ask the side effects to be workable.

Email outbox: August 15th

Good Morning:

Today the port goes in and the biopsy is done on the lymph node. Thank you in advance that the Cancer is only in the right breast.

Thank you that you are in the midst of me, that I will be an encouragement to those around me. You are a victorious warrior and I will be healed for you always win the battles. You will exult over me with joy and you are quiet in your love for me - gentle songs of the birds and soft breezes that touch my face - the flowers in the fields, yes you are quiet in your love for me. You will rejoice over me with singing and I shall listen today for your songs of love and hope and peace and encouragement. (Based on Zeph. 3:17)

T.

Email outbox: August 16th

Good Evening:

An update from today: Everything went well. God is so good to/for His children! The first thing was removing the centennial lymph node and the two on either side. It really hurt when the radiologist put the radioactive dye in five (yes, five!) areas in the lymph node and the dye was moving through the tissue. The whole thing lasted about five minutes.

These lymph nodes will be where the biopsy will take place and I should know Thursday when I see Dr. Paulishak at ten. Then I waited about forty-five minutes for surgery to remove the lymph nodes for the biopsy and to place the port. The port is located on my left side where the neck and chest areas meet near the shoulder blade, a rather large ball looking thing unlike the stent. Maybe it's just the bandages at this point. I am a little sore where they took out the lymph nodes. Also on Thursday, I will have this surgery looked at and be given the OK to start chemo this Friday at nine.

Today as I was waiting I was praying for you, some as individuals and others as groups. I really believe this is larger than just asking for prayer and being part of a prayer chain. I really sense that what God has started to do and will accomplish in the end is big. I am thankful to be a part of it and it includes all of us that are on this journey together not only for you on this email but also for other prayer chains. My sister, Leigh Ann, Jason and his wife Tara have put me on theirs. Other churches too! I think it is exciting! I think of the movie *A Wonderful Life* with Jimmy Stewart. You never know how or whom your life may touch for God's glory.

James 5:16

T.

Email inbox: from my daughter-in-law Tara.

Glad you are home and feeling well, one step to the end!

Prayer Journal:
August 17th

"And all things you ask in prayer, believing you shall receive." Matthew 21:22

I am standing on God's word. HIS word is truth. John 1:14 says this sickness will not end in death.

Thank you, Abba Father for healing for me. I pray the side effects will be minimal, that I will rest and be grateful for the quiet times during these next six months.

"I want to dwell in beauty." (Phil 4:8)

Email outbox: August 18th

Good Evening:

Tomorrow at nine, I have my first chemo treatment (rather a strange word for chemo. I think of a spa when I think of treatment). I think there is way too much information out there. If all the side effects happen to me I will be like the men on the Bataan Death March during WWII. My doctors have assured me that no one has had all side effects and the worst will be few and short lived if at all. When they called to confirm the time I asked how long and they said three hours! Some is paperwork and they don't mix the chemicals of the chemo (poison) until you walk in the door. I think I will take a Scrabble game in case Cindy Vaughn (who is taking me) wants to play.

And I read 2 Chronicles 6:1; *"The Lord has said that he would dwell in the thick dark cloud."*

These next six months will be like a thick darkness at times and God said He will dwell with me. I must remember - He made the rainbow.

Again and always I thank you for your prayers, smiles, and encouragement and just being you.

Romans 11:33

T.

Email outbox: August 18th

Good Morning:

This morning as I walked Annie I prayed for you: Healing for some, stronger healthy marriages for those of you who are married. That God would heal families, give back the years the locusts have eaten for various reasons and most importantly that each of you would have a closer, deeper walk with our Lord this coming year.

Psalm 40:1-3

T.

Email outbox: August 19th

Today is one of seven chemo treatments.

"He will arise and shepherd his flock in the strength of the Lord." (Micah 5:4)

The expression "shepherd" in Greek, means to do everything expected of a shepherd: To guide, to watch, to preserve, to restore, to tend, as well as feed.

"Free me from the trap that is set for me, for you are my refuge." (Psalm 31:4)

Father God, please free me from the trap of side effects of chemo.

"'For you are my refuge.' What an inexpressible sweetness is to be found in these few words! How joyfully may we encounter toils, and cheerfully may we endure suffering when we can lay hold upon celestial strength." (Morning and Evening by Charles H. Spurgeon, page 465)

Email outbox: August 19th

Good Evening:

This could be long but, hey! My time in chemo was three hours! When I got there I had to register. You would think will all the papers they have on me... Oh well. That took ten minutes, then I was shown into the chemo lab and I had to choose a reclining chair. I had visions of everyone in a circle facing each other like group therapy in a movie, "Hi, my name is Terry and I have Cancer..." but I was wrong. The chairs were in rows of four to a row with bookcases that had books and blankets in them. There were a few curtains that you could pull if needed between the chairs. All rather homey and civil.

I had the same nurse all morning. Ann. She started the anti-nausea drip and then a small drip of antibiotics. While those where going through the port my chemo was being mixed. At 10:15 the chemo began, a red colored one that took twenty minutes, then a clear one that took one hour.
Cindy talked and I read some of my truth cards, then we played Scrabble. I told Jason about our game and he called me the queen of the three letter words - cat, hat, dog... You've got the idea. The letters got askew and then my nurse Ann came back to check on me and saw the letters and said we were cheating with a new language. Cindy and I laughed and told her the problem... It did look pretty funny. We laughed a lot and I drank lots of water to start washing the chemo out of me. I was the only one drinking water or anything for that matter. Strange, I thought. Why was I the only one that wanted to get it out!

I told Ann in the beginning I would rather be in a den of rattlesnakes and she said she never thought of it like that. Later on in the morning she asked me how the rattlesnakes were doing as she looked at the drip and checked the numbers. I said, "Not bad, maybe the den of snakes would be worse." She just smiled.

When we were leaving, Cindy and I were talking about Emerson, my two-and-a-half year old granddaughter and how she says, "I've got it," as she climbs into her car seat by herself. Ann heard us and as I was showing her pictures of Emerson on my phone, she said, "I don't know you well, as we have just met, but I have a feeling your granddaughter is going to be as independent as you are." I smiled and said, "I hope so."

That morning for breakfast I had yogurt, cereal, fruit, and a slice of homemade zucchini bread that a dear friend made. Cindy and I went to lunch afterwards at Panera's. I had a bowl of chicken noodle soup and an apple salad. As I type this I am eating roasted veggies and another slice of zucchini bread with yogurt and hot tea. I have beans soaking to make bean soup tomorrow. All this is to let you know I am eating and eat well - a must if you are on chemo.

I saw a friend yesterday and I told him how happy I was. I was even laughing more than usual. Did he think I was weird? That I didn't want to be arrogant or presume anything? He said, "Either a loony person would say that or someone with a close walk with God. You are number two. You are a witness for Him."

That being said I would never be able to laugh without your prayers. I know God hears prayers. To name a few:

"But He hears the prayers of the righteous." Proverbs 15:29b

"Then the Lord appeared to Solomon at night and said to him, 'I have heard your prayer, and have chosen this place for Myself as a house of sacrifice'." 2 Chronicles 7:12.

"And when He had taken the book the four living creatures and the twenty-four elders fell down before the Lamb, having each one a harp, and golden bowls full of incense, which are the prayers of the saints." Revelations 5:8.

Today's only side effect so far is that my eyes ache, like when I don't wear my sunglasses in the bright sun. They are okay now. And I have a headache running across my forehead that started two hours ago.

I do enjoy praying for all of you. That is the very least I can do for you as you pray for me.

"Be anxious for nothing, but in everything by prayer and supplication with thanksgiving let your requests be made known to God. And the peace of God which surpasses all comprehension shall guard your hearts and your minds in Christ Jesus." Philippians 4:6-7.

T.

Email inbox: from Ron Salvanggio

People like you that are praying and thinking of us while fighting your own battles are a rare and wonderful treat.

Email outbox: August 21st

Good Morning:

Yesterday I got "the shot" – Neulasta - to start the release of white blood cells from the bones. I did take a Clarion as it somehow helps the bone pain that could start and last two or three days. As of yet nothing. Thank you for your faithful praying for me!! The Clarion label says non-drowsy, but that is a lie to my body! Yesterday afternoon I took a nap... real sleep, shocking I know. And last night at work I had a hot flash that was the combination of all the hot flashes I had years ago.... my face was like an apple! And the Clarion was doing its job it says it doesn't do...

Once again, I walked around the Flying W with our miniature donkey Chloe for the kids to pet and take pictures with, blinking my eyes to stay awake... by sevenish all was back to normal.

As I walked my dog Annie this morning I prayed for you. Seems like that is the time the Lord is having me pray for you... ah, quiet, peaceful. The sun is just breaking through the clouds and there was the left-over smell of the rain from last night... life is good, isn't it???

I prayed some things I read this morning from Morning and Evening, Springs in the Desert and a new one that a dear friend gave me. Jesus Calling (amazing book).

"I prayed for you, 'That the Lord would show you his unsearchable riches that He has for each of you... My

Master has riches of happiness to give you now... to lay down in green pastures, lead you beside quiet waters, there is no music like the music of His pipe...'" (From Morning and Evening by Charles H. Spurgeon, page 471)

"O LORD, the God of Israel, there is no God like Thee in heaven above or on earth beneath, who art keeping covenant and showing loving kindness to Thy servants who walk before Thee with all their heart." 1 Kings 8:23

I pray Jesus I will have an open and willing heart as we walk together on this road called Cancer. You have made a covenant with me and you have shown loving kindness to me your daughter in the past and you will continue to do so as you can not lie. (Based on Hebrews 6:18)

"And You do not change." (Hebrews 13:8)

"He brought me forth also into a large place; He delivered me because he delighted in me (Psalm 18:19) *and what is this large place? What can it be but God himself."* (From Streams in the Desert, page 250)

As some of you know I have struggled with love and trust from God and I think this Cancer journey He has placed me on is showing me His great love for me. It is all so exciting isn't it?! I am asking for a bold prayer that the Cancer will be gone after chemo... no need for surgery? Not that I mind the loss of the right breast but the evasiveness of it all.

Have a great day with Jesus as He is lifting you with eagles' wings to be with Him.

T.

Email inbox: from Bonnie McGowan

Oh Terry, this is so encouraging and such a blessing. You are a true example of one walking with the Lord and trusting in Him. Thank you for sharing with us, praying for us, and encouraging us.

From my Prayer Journal
August 22nd

The quiet of the early morning - to be still and know you are God. You, oh God, the great and only I AM cares for me and is holding me up with your Righteous Right Hand. Thank you and praise you. Please encourage and bless those who are praying for me.

Email outbox: August 24th

Good Morning to a faithful prayer group:

A few days ago they took blood at Dr Hoyer's office for a special test to see if I might have to have the left breast removed at time of surgery when they remove the right one due to Cancer in the family history. The testing company called yesterday and said that my insurance would not pay for the test because there was no paperwork to go with the request. I am meeting with Teresa, a genetic counselor recommended by Dr. Hoyer next week to see if the test is needed. Please pray that it will be clear to all what is needs to be done. I am praying that the chemo will do its job (and will cure all Cancer). Period.

Please also be praying for three women who were in the chemo lab with me on Friday and then again on Saturday when I went to get the shot. They were getting chemo both days. And please also pray for my daughter-in law Tara's uncle Kip who also has Cancer. Thank you!

Early this morning it was peaceful with a warm breeze coming in the windows. As I was reading my Bible and touching the pages, I said to myself; "Oh God's word IS truth and there is nothing like it."

Within the pages of my Bible I have copies of devotionals I have read for one of those fox hole times of needed prayer or just quiet times with the Lord. This morning was the latter. A quiet time. I would like to share it with you.

"Iguazu Falls on the border of Brazil and Argentina is a spectacular waterfall system of 1.67 miles on the Iguazu River.

Etched on a rock wall below one of the falls are the words from Psalm 93:4 'Mightier than the thunders of many waters, mightier than the waves of the sea, the LORD on high is mighty.' Below this phrase are the words: 'God is always greater than all of our troubles.'

Below it are these words: 'God is always greater than all our troubles.' This ended with, 'Never measure God's unlimited power by your limited expectations.'" (From Daily Bread)

Thank you all for praying and walking this journey with me. Each day is new and filled with His Ahhhh moments and healing.

"The Lord who is able to do exceeding abundantly above all that we ask or think." (Ephesians. 3:20)

T.

From my Prayer Journal
August 25th

Thank you Lord that I am *"Shut up into faith"* (Gal.3:23) on this journey we are on together - that you will show me blessings, help, insights that would never have happened. I want others to see you, not me. I see me as a sheep walking close to her shepherd's side with his hand on her head. I am grateful I am yours. Oh, the depth of love you have for me - there is no measure.

Email outbox: August 27th

Good Morning:

I had blood work on Thursday to check the counts of red and white cells to see if the chemo needs to adjusted for #2. That will be Friday the 2nd at 9:30.

Thank you in advance for praying for that! These past few days have been mentally hard. I have talked, not by choice, to others who have family members who are at the present time doing chemo and they had horror stories to tell me. I found myself feeling very guilty from feeling so good. And with #2 next week I think, "Could the rug be pulled out"?

But then there is the flip side of doing good and that is a good thing: I had a massage last week and Helen (a very strong Christian) was working on my feet and told me that this is the first time ever that my nerves are working as they should and I look better than ever. I told her it was a God thing and she agreed. And one of our employees told me that because I am so open about all of this and talk about what God is doing in my life she knows that the physical issues she is facing will work out ok.

"For Thou has been my help and in the shadow of Thy wings I sing for joy."

Oh Jesus, the sparkle you add is exciting and fun like the sparkle on a little girl's shoes. I smile as I walk along with you. I want sparkle in my life on this journey of Cancer. Take away the fear of facing chemo #2. Please, no side effects. Amen.

"And He took him aside from the multitude." (Mark 7:33)

"I see Paul in prison, writing a document and signing his name not as the prisoner of Fetus, nor of Caesar; not the victim of the Sanhedrin; but the ... 'prisoner of the Lord.' He saw only the hand of God in it all. To him the prison becomes a palace. Its corridors ring with shouts of triumphant praise and joy.

For twelve long years Bunyan's (the author of Pilgrim's Progress) lips were silenced in Bedford jail... He says, 'I was at home in prison and I sat me down and wrote and wrote, for joy did make me write.'" (From Streams in the Desert, page 257)

Oh Father God, the Great I Am, I sense you have taken me also from the multitude. Oh, that I would see this journey of Cancer. We are together as Paul the Apostle and Bunyan did theirs, as a time of adding sparkle to my daily life and praise to You, that at the end you will say to me, "Well done, My child".

Please be praying for a woman named Betty. I met her and her husband in Dr. Hoyer's office. She was one of the horror stories I heard about. I told her and her husband I would be praying and would ask you to pray too. There were tears in their eyes that said "Thank you".

Have a wonderful week, watching Jesus add sparkle to your life.

T.

Email inbox: From Ron Salvanggio:

Keep doing ALL the things you need to do to stay healthy. The challenge is that you are working to kill the Cancer while staying healthy. An interesting battle, to say the least.

From my Prayer Journal
August 28th

"Lift up the light of Thy countenance upon us, O Lord!"
(Psalm 4:6b)

When I read that this morning my spirit leaped for joy knowing the side effects will be nothing for the duration of chemo. Thank you, Jesus. I am grateful your hand is on the head of me as we walk together on this journey. There will be a joyful ending for Your glory.

Oh Jesus, I do want everyone to see you in me. Perhaps this is leading me to a field of ministry for you. I ask that I will be able to pray and hopefully talk to others on Friday in the chemo lab - to share you. Thank you.

Email outbox: August 30th

Good Evening:

This a long one. Get a cup of coffee and get comfy - feet up, etc...

I saw Dr. Hoyer's assistant John today to go over blood work from last week and talk about how I did with chemo #1. The blood showed my white counts were a little low (if I wasn't doing chemo they wouldn't have been recorded).

The shot on Saturday got them back to normal. That is why I was tired. I asked if it was true that how I reacted the first time will be how I react through the rest. He said yes, that I would be a little tired, my eyes tired and achy.

I need to be careful as in the seventh to tenth day I can bleed if I get cut, which I did do. The small cut bled for two days on my arm but it is ok today. I told John that I was a Christian and that God was doing amazing things in me through this Cancer journey. He said that those like me who are in tune with their spiritual side do far better than those who aren't. He told me I was going to do fine since I was grabbing the bull by the horns and have a very positive attitude. "This is a bump in the road to get over and get on with your life." I agreed with him when he said that.

I told him when I first learned that I had Cancer my first thought was, "Oh my hair will fall out, a sign that something is very wrong going on inside."

A friend told me to look at the positive. Hair is fast-growing cells and always falling out and growing back. Cancer cells are fast-growing and spreading so if the hair is falling out the chemo is doing its job as the Cancer cells are dying too. So I can't wait for the hair to start falling out!

He said that is a great example of how I am looking at this. I also told him how I have gotten cards from people who won't say the word CANCER and I threw them in the trash. He laughed and said that is their problem, not mine. I agreed.

Thursday I have blood work at nine for this chemo on Friday to see if there need to be any adjustments made, then at 9:30 I am to talk to a woman about having a blood test called a BRAC analysis done to see what is the possibility of also having to have the left breast removed at time of surgery due to a history of Cancer in the family. Please pray that it will be very clear if there needs to be a test or not.

Friday at 9:30 is Chemo #2. Please pray that it is true how it went the first time will be the same or better. Deena is stopping by. It will be fun to play our second Scrabble game. I wonder if she can get above three letter words? And also pray for the people who will be there, that Deena and I will be good witnesses for the Lord. Pray for them and maybe talk to them. How cool would that be?

"There he proved them." (Exodus 15:25)

"He wants us to be not hothouse plants, but storm-beaten oaks; not sand dunes driven with every gust of wind, but granite rocks, withstanding the fiercest storms... Oh happy are we if the hurricanes that ripple life's unquiet sea have the effect of making Jesus more precious. Better the storm with Christ than smooth waters without Him." (Streams in the Desert, page 259)

I see myself as a sheep walking close to my Shepherd with His hand on my head as we walk down the road. I know He is in control and prayerfully the chemo times coming will be uneventful for my body. I don't want to be overly confident, but, that I can and will be a witness He will be smiling about. I would like to thank whoever gave a picture of a cowboy on horseback carrying a calf in a storm. Regarding the painting, there is a quote from Isaiah 46:6 that I would like to close with:

"I have made you and I will carry you; and I will sustain you and I will rescue you."

Sleep well in the arms of Jesus,

T.

From my Prayer Journal
August 31st

A friend gave me Psalm 118:17 after reading my email about chemo #2.

"I shall not die but live and declare the works of the Lord."

CHAPTER 3 - SEPTEMBER

Email outbox: September 1st

After talking to my genetic counselor Teresa for over an hour she doesn't think it is necessary for me to have the BRAC testing. Even though there is a history of Cancer in my family there is no Ovarian Cancer which is a huge sign along with Breast Cancer (need both). There is a possibility that my grandmother had Breast Cancer but nothing concrete to speak of, only rumors.

There are three kinds of my Cancer:

The first is sporadic, where 80% of the Cancer is. No reason why someone gets it, but does.

The second is caused by familial genes and the environment. 15 - 20 % of the gene could be there but not sure. A smoker with Lung Cancer is an example of environment...

Teresa thinks I am in this category. I could have the gene, but not sure from a generation or two back...

The third cause is hereditary. 10% of people have this. The BRAC test would show a hereditary gene MAYBE... there is an 87% possibility that the test will come back negative with me...

That leaves a 13% possibility that it could be positive and from an unknown area since I have no proven history of Ovarian Cancer in the family. Teresa thinks it would be money not spent wisely as the insurance company would not pay for my test. She has been doing this for ten years and in that time she has come across only four people that needed the test.

My blood was drawn to see if the chemo needs to be adjusted tomorrow and if my blood is ok to take in the chemo. I told Teresa I hated to complain about my "small effects of achy eyes, off and on headaches and constipation for two days. She looked me straight in the eyes and said, "There are no small effects with chemo. You are handling it with grace and style."

Thank you for your prayers and praying. Will give you an update tomorrow sometime.

You are living James 5:16 for me!

T.

September 1st
Email inbox: from Jason

"This is another day O Lord. I know not what it will bring forth, but make me ready, Lord, for whatever it may be. If I am to stand up help me stand bravely. If I am to sit still, help me to sit quietly. If I am to lie low, let me do it patiently. If I am to do nothing, let me do it gallantly. Make

these more than words. And give me the Spirit of Jesus. Amen." (From the Book of Common Prayer)

"I love the Lord, because He hears my voice and my supplications. Because he has inclined His ear to me, therefore I shall call upon Him as long as I live." (Psalm 116:1-2)

We love you and are praying for you!

From my Prayer Journal
September 2nd

Today is chemo #2.

"When thou walkest through the fire thou shall not be burned." (Isaiah 43:2)

"My safety is in the stillness of soul. If I exchange the principle of faith for that of fear I shall be hurt by the flames and anguish and disappointment will be the result... moreover, God will be disappointed if I break down. Testing is proof of His love and confidence and who can tell what pleasure our steadfastness and stillness give Him? God has confidence in us that He believes we are strong enough to endure: that we shall be true to Him even when He has left us without outward evidence of His care and seemingly at the mercy of His adversaries. If He increases the trials it is an expression of confidence in us and proof that He is looking to us to glorify Him in yet hotter fires which He is calling us to pass. O God make me a child of quietness." (From Springs in the Valley, page 260).

Email outbox: September 2nd

Good Afternoon:

All is well. NO side effects! Deena and I went to lunch, then I had to run to the Flying W. Just got home. God is good. I am so sorry all these past years of my doubting Him.

I talked to Jason after leaving the hospital and told him I hope and pray everyone will continue to pray for me even though I am doing great. I know God is the one who is doing all this in my life but I also know prayer works and is needed and God hears and answers prayer. So don't stop praying for me! I know I have a mighty band of prayer warriors in the full armor of God.

In the movie *Braveheart* there is a scene where William Wallace is on a hill with his men in full battle dress and he puts his sword up and out and yells, *"Freedom"* and with that cry, his men run forward into battle. That is what you are doing for me!

Thank you!

Yesterday my hair started falling out just like the book said it would do on day fourteen. This morning when I took my dog Annie for a walk and was praying for you, I pulled out hair and threw it into the gentle breeze that was blowing. Laughing, I told God, "Here is building material for the birds" and thanked Him that my hair was falling out and that the chemo was doing its job.

I went to the Chuckwagon stores at Flying W to water the flowers and clean a little before I left for Memorial Hospital. I was joined by Phyllis, one of my teacher friends. I told her about my hair falling out and asked if I should just cut it off and be done with it. She said, "Let's do it now!" So we did! She took some scissors and cut two or three inches all over.

I now look like a nice Jewish woman in Dachau. I can't lose any more weight! Only two pounds in two weeks, but I am borderline and the nurse, Michelle, told me it wouldn't be good if they had to adjust the chemo by going lower or higher, so I can't gain a lot. I have a 5% margin to work in. Please pray accordingly.

As Isaiah says in 55:11: *"So shall My word be which goes forth from My mouth; it shall not return to Me empty, without accomplishing what I desire, and without succeeding in the matter for which I sent it."*

In the chemo lab Deena and I read my Bible (she read it out loud) and we prayed. We were able to share our faith with two of the nurses (both Christians we found out) and I was able to talk to one of the women getting chemo (a pleasant chat but I know she heard Deena and I talking - a good thing).

Deena and I played Scrabble for two hours!!! Sure made the time go by. I think we have a tie for the "Queen of Three Letter Words" but we both did come up with a few four letter ones (leaf, home) to give you an idea of our spelling ability.

Afterwards Deena and I went to a Panera's restaurant. I had a WHOLE salad and a WHOLE sandwich (are you proud of me? And now I am having a trail bar).

Yesterday, Teresa also told me there are two kinds of Cancer patients: one who lives their Cancer and one who lives their life. She said I was number two. And for her to see my faith was delightful. Thank you, Lord!

This is what I prayed this morning before going for chemo:

"Lord, help me to stand if needed. May I sit quietly as you continue to heal me. To lie low as you give me directions on this road we are walking together - to do nothing so you will get all the glory and not me.'

Have a great weekend. You ARE the best!!!

T.

Email Outbox: September 3rd

The following coincides with my thoughts.

"This is a time of praise and thanksgiving to you o Lord, The Great I Am. You are and do your names. You are: The Creator, Elohim... you made heaven and earth and you made me; The God Most High, El Elyon... the God I Worship; The God Who Sees, El Roi... You see all the time." (Psalm 44:12, Psalm 139:1-2)

"The All Sufficient One; The El Saddai... my protector, the unconditional lover of my soul... You have me when I have failed. The Lord, Adonai... You are Lord and Master... total possession of me and my total submission to Him as Lord and Master... until now I didn't know what that meant The Self-existent one: Jehovah...You meet the needs of those He created in His Image... you have constantly met my needs better in so many areas of my life. Thank you. The Lord Heals; Jehovah -Rapha... I could list what huge things you have healed me from physical and mental but this Cancer journey is different, deeper, more profound. The Lord is My Banner: Jehovah-Nissi; The Lord is the first to fight my battles. The Lord Who Sanctifies You; Jehovah-Mekaddishkem. He bore me on eagles wings and brought me to Himself to worship Him in Spirit and Truth through Jesus Christ, The Lord is Peace; Lehovah-Shalom... when the hour is dark and the situation desperate, we long for God's peace...the only true peace is in the right relationship with God. The Lord of Hosts; Jehovah-Sabaoth... when my strength is gone and need of deliverance I seek you. The Lord is my Shepherd; Jehovah-Raah... I like a sheep, if not under the constant care of a shepherd will go the wrong way, unaware of the dangers at hand. I am glad I know His voice as I am on this Cancer journey with Him. The Lord of Righteousness; Jehovah-Tsidkenu... I can be right with God due to a new heart. I am so grateful that You O Lord took me out of the pit and gave me a new song." (Based on *Lord I Want To Know You* by Kay Arthur)

"The Lord is there. Jehovah-Shammah. As Corrie Ten Boom (a Dutch Christian who hid Jews in a secret room, was captured and placed in a concentration camp) said, *"There is no pit that God is not deeper still."*

I stand in awe of You O Lord. Thank you that the first two chemo treatments and shots the day after were perfect. While going to work on both Friday afternoons there was a rainbow. Thank you! The Lamb of God who loves us more than life itself. Jesus died on the cross for me and you. Holy Holy Holy are You, O Lord. Thank you for this Cancer journey we are on together. Thank you for the mighty prayer warriors you have given me to hold me along the way as they charge head first into the enemy lines with prayer. Please bless them, protect them, and answer all spoken and unspoken prayer requests. I wanted to share a huge praise and thanks to God for what He is doing!! It is a glorious time isn't it?

September 3rd
Email inbox: from Bonnie McGowan

Oh Terry, you just made me cry. This is the same God The Father, God The Son, and God The Holy Spirit that belongs to me. He guides me and directs me. He is my Creator, (He knows me by name... even before the creation of the earth). He is my Savior, Redeemer, Protector, Counselor, Healer, Provider, Everlasting Father, Prince of Peace - no matter what I go through or have gone through, all I have to do is look back and see with tears in my eyes what He has done for me.

Terry, you are a living testimony of our Lord and Savior Jesus Christ and how He rescued you and saved you. He loves us so much. In the ups and downs - he is always there - never to leave or forsake us. God is using you in a very special way and we may never know all that He is doing to bring others to Himself in this Cancer Journey that you are on with Him. Thank you for honoring and glorying the Lord through it all. As we worship our Lord and Savior

Jesus Christ tomorrow, I'm praying you'll be blessed and refreshed. I know I will. Praying for you.

From my Prayer Journal
September 4th

"In closeness to Me, you are safe. In the intimacy of My Presence you are energized. When you commune with Me in the garden of your heart, both you and I are blessed. This is My way of living in the world - through you! Together we will push back the darkness. For I am the Light of the world. (Based on Psalm 32:7; Genesis 3:8-9; John 8:12 from Jesus Calling, page 259)

Thank you, Jesus. I am safe with you and in the closeness of Your Presence I am energized. Growing and at peace, I pray my emails to the prayer warriors that You have given me are encouraging them on their walk with you.

"And when you hear the sound of the trumpet, and the people shall shout with a great shout; and the walls of the city shall fall down flat and the people shall ascend up every man straight before him." (Joshua 6:5)

"The shout of steadfast faith is in direct contrast to the moans of waivering faith and to the wails of discouraged hearts.... the shout did cause the wall to fall but it was a shout of faith on the Authority of God's Word alone to claim a promised victory, while there was none in sight.... God had declared that He had given them the city, and

faith reckoned that to be true." (From Streams in the Desert, page 265)

Thank you Lord, that this journey of Cancer is a walk of faith for I know you are healing me and true there will be a joyous end. It is taking a long time with chemo, surgery, and radiation for there is much to heal. I ask that I will be an encouragement to those who are praying for me and others at the chemo lab and doctor's office.

September 4th
Email inbox: from Sherry Brian

As I prayed last night on the drive home for the healing touch of Jesus to permeate every portion of Your Life the verse or scripture that we discussed (at the ranch) came to me again. It is Mark 16:17-18. Just before those verses, after His resurrection, Jesus appeared to the eleven to soundly rebuke their unbelief and hardness of heart.

I can't even imagine how they felt after they witnessed the death of Jesus. How could they even dare to hope or believe those who told them he was alive? When he commanded them to go into all the world and preach the gospel to everyone who believed what they told them and that those who got baptized would be saved - and those who refused to believe would be condemned, they must've feared for their own lives.

The Bible doesn't say so, but at least some of them must've wanted to back-peddle and go back to their old lives. That's when he said, *"And those signs will follow those of you who believe in MY name you will cast out demons, speak with new tongues, take up serpents, and if you drink anything deadly, it will by no means hurt you. You will lay hands on the sick, and they will recover."*

Lord Jesus. Terry loves you. She is a living example of Your promise that the poisonous drink of chemotherapy will NOT harm her. She is your servant, Father.

Thank you for healing her completely and for Your plan to use her to heal others.

In Jesus name - Amen.

Email inbox: from Ruth Mott

What a wonderful tribute to our God! I am thanking Him that you are able to give Him such praise and worship in the midst of such a deep trial. You are an inspiration and example to me. I am praying Acts 3:16 for you, dear friend.

Email outbox: September 8th

Good Morning:

This coming Tuesday, September 13th, I meet with Dr. Hoyer's assistant John to discuss chemo #2 and to talk about round #2 that begins at the end of October.

I have two drug choices: Taxol or Taxotere. I can't remember which is which, but one I would take weekly for twelve weeks and the other I would take every three weeks over a period of twelve weeks. As of now I am going to take one every three weeks for twelve weeks but I want to be sure that is the right choice. They both can have dreadful side effects. I must remember this round has bad effects too, but God is faithful to His Word and I have had very small to no side effects.

I am trusting God that #3 and #4 of this round of chemo will be uneventful (Sept. 16th and 30th). I am trusting God that round #2 starting at the end of October will be uneventful as well.

"They will pick up serpents, and if they drink deadly poison it will not hurt them." Mark 16:18

Chemo is a poison (I think). I am standing on God's Word that this poison of chemo that is killing the Cancer will continue to have no side effects on me. I don't know why God allows some with Cancer to suffer and oftentimes die while others like me do so well and in the end are healed.

"For My thoughts are not your thoughts, nor are your ways My ways, say the LORD." Isaiah 55:8

And it is very exciting the lump (tumor) is getting smaller! And I am looking more and more like Yul Brynner, thinking of him dancing with Deborah Kerr in the movie *"The King and I"* dancing to *"Shall We Dance"* as the hair falls out, the lump gets smaller and Cancer is being killed off...

Oh happy day! *"Trust in the LORD with all your heart and lean not on your own understanding; In all your ways acknowledge Him, And He will direct your paths."* Proverbs:3,5,6

T.

From my Prayer Journal
September 7th

The side effects for round #2 can be numbness in the hands and feet and nails falling off. I started to panic but then remembered Mark 16:17b *"...and if they drink any deadly poison, it shall not hurt them."*

The Enemy wants me to panic but he knows I believe and stand on the truth of God's Word not the facts or maybes in medicine. I am a daughter of the Living God, the Great I Am. Mark 16 17-18 is truth and so is Isaiah 41:10.

From my Prayer Journal
September 9th

Psalm 32:7 says, *"Thou aren't my hiding place; Thou dost preserve me from trouble; Thou dost surround me with songs of deliverance."*

Thank you, Jesus that You are healing me in your time. You chose the team of doctors, the process and length of time needed. I do trust you absolutely and I am resting in your strength moment by moment. Your peace, love, healing, and grace are abiding in me – You, Oh Lord, are worthy to be praised.

From my Prayer Journal
September 10th

"The Lord will perfect that which concerns me." (Psalm 138:8)

"There is a divine mystery in suffering, a strange and supernatural power in it, which has never been fathomed by human reason. When the suffering soul reaches a calm sweet carelessness, when it can inwardly smile at its own suffering, and does not even ask God to deliver it from suffering, then it has wrought its blessed ministry; then patience has its perfect work; then the crucifixion begins to weave itself into a crown.

It is in this state of perfection of suffering that the Holy Spirit works many marvelous things in our souls. A quietness of eternity settles down into the whole being; the tongue grows still and has but few words to say; it stops asking God questions; it stops crying, 'Why hast thou forsaken me?'

The imagination stops building air castles or running off on foolish lines; for let the circumstances be what they may, it seeks only for God and His will, and it feels assured that God is making everything in the universe, good or bad, past or present, work together for its good."

"The greatest thing is to suffer without being discouraged." (From Streams in the Desert, page 271)

Thank you Abba Father, for giving me the ability to laugh at the enemy - to rejoice with Holy laugher as the enemy pounds at the gate knowing you are standing between me and Cancer - you are healing me and there will be a joyful end!

Thank you, Holy Spirit for working many marvelous things in my soul. You will never forsake me - you are carrying me - there is only one set of footprints in the sand. I know you have everything in the universe - good, bad, past, present working together for my good. Praise you for you are worthy of praise. You are King of Kings and Lord of Lords, You are the Great I Am, The Shepherd of my soul. I am a sheep of Your flock.

Email outbox: September 13th

Good Afternoon:

I saw Dr Hoyer's assistant John again this morning. He is pleased at how well I am doing. The lump is going down. It isn't shrinking as a whole but it is "swiss-cheesing" and getting smaller but in more than one place. This to me is a sure sign I will need surgery to make sure it is all gone. When the lump does this there is a good chance the Cancer can go into the margins.

When I saw Dr. Paulishak to drain the area of lymph nodes that was removed she said I will need surgery because there will need to be a biopsy to make sure the Cancer is gone and the only way to do that is to remove the breast.

On a lighter note, I was born a blonde and by the time I entered college it started to turn dark. I then started to color my hair to keep it blonde. As I got older and after my son Jason was born, my hair was really dark so I kept coloring it. When my hair started to fall out, the first layer was the coloring. Then the natural dark started coming out. I threw those layers to the birds and cleaned out the bath tub a few times. Now what is left is blonde - fuzzy roots but blonde! How cool is that? I am a blonde.

Today at Dr. Hoyer's office, two nurses and Dr. Hoyer's assistant John said they always are glad to see me because I am so uplifting for them all. Sherri (Dr. Hoyer's head nurse) told me this has been a hard year due to some hard losses. (I assume that means the deaths of some of their patients.) Two staff members are in counseling, like soldiers suffering from post traumatic stress syndrome. Please pray for those in that office. As I was leaving they asked when I was coming back.

Thank you, Jesus they are seeing you!

Closing thought:

There is a sign setting on a table in Dr Hoyer's office:

"Life is not waiting for the storm to pass. It is learning to dance in the rain."

Praying for you,

T.

Email outbox: September 15th

Good Morning:

This Friday, September the 16th, is chemo #3. Please pray for no side-effects and no bone pain after the shot and that I will be a good witness of Jesus.

In the past seven to ten days out from chemo #2 when I could bleed if I got cut, I only hurt my arms twice. The first was on Saturday night. I ran into a closed gate at work. It was very dark. A small amount of skin was removed from my arm.

This morning when I was trimming back the flowers at the Flying W, I hit my arm with the tip of the clippers (I know you are laughing and shaking your heads thinking, "Will she ever act like a girl and slow down"?). The bleeding was slight both times. Thank you for your prayers.

"I will sing of your love and justice." (Psalm 101:1)

"Faith triumphs in trial. When reason is thrust into the inner prison, with her feet fastened in the stocks, faith makes the dungeon wall ring with her merry notes as she cries, "I will sing of Your love and Justices. To You, O LORD, I will sing praise." Faith pulls the dark mask from the face of trouble, and discovers the angel beneath."

60

(From Morning and Evening by Charles H. Spurgeon, page 513)

"Receive My Peace. It is My continual gift to you. The best way to receive this gift is to set quietly in My Presence, trusting Me in every area of your life. Quietness and trust accomplish far more than you can imagine: not only in you, but also on earth and heaven. When you trust Me in a given area, you release the problem or person into My care. Living close to Me is a sure defense against evil." (Based on John 14:27; Isaiah - 30:15; 2 Corinthians 10:4 from Jesus Calling, page 267)

Thank you, O LORD, for the faith you have given me to sing on this journey of Cancer YOU and I are on. Trust and Faith are mighty oak trees that I can set under as I receive Your peace, quietness and trust that accomplish more than I can imagine. As I face chemo #3 on Friday I shall think of you and I having a lovely picnic under the large oak trees laughing and chatting. Thank you, Jesus.

Dear Prayer Warriors; Will you join me for the picnic under the oak tress of Trust and Faith with Jesus on Friday Morning?

You are living James 5:16, Thank you

T.

**From my Prayer Journal
September 16th**

Today is chemo #3. I ask once again for no side effects and that when I weigh in I will be 122 or above. Please.

"Though I may lead you along paths that feel alien to you, trust that I know what I am doing. If you follow Me whole heartedly you will discover facets of yourself that were previously hidden. I know you intimately - far better than you know yourself. In union with me you are complete. In closeness to Me, you are transformed more and more into the one I designed you to be. (Based on Psalm 139:13-16; 2 Corinthians 3:17-18 - from Jesus Calling, page 271)

Oh Jesus, thank you for this journey of Cancer you and I are on. It's alien and strange to me but I am trusting you with each step. I am excited to discover facets about myself that have been hidden and that on this journey you are designing me to be the person you know I am. Thank you that after it is over, (the end of March?) there will be a joyous end and I will be free to be me- to dance in the rain.

Email outbox: September 16th

Good Evening (this is a long one!):

Again, I would like to thank you for praying and please continue to do so. I would never be this at-ease with the side effects without your prayers...

Things I found out: I need to keep my weight up all along and not eat like a pregnant elephant ready to drop in 24 hours like I did yesterday.

The reason I need to stay between 122 and 127 is due to the chemo mix. Being thin, slight, and small (words the nurse used to describe me) is a health issue for my body. My body is working double time to stay healthy. At the doctor's office I weighed in at 124.8 yesterday morning. I was at 120 the day before so I ate like an elephant with twins. It is harder for a thin person to stay healthy while fighting off Cancer and the effects of chemo. Most people have five to ten pounds they can afford to lose. I don't (thanks to my dog Annie). She demands a walk for her potty duties and can't/won't go in the yard!

This is a healthy loss of weight for me. I weighed 140 a year ago before "Queen" Annie arrived. It took about seven months to drop the weight and I did eat. My red and white blood cells were healthy and strong.

My potassium level is between 3.5 and 4.5. I am at 3.5 so off to the store not only for bananas, but oranges and dried apricots (I heard they are good).

The lump is starting to get smaller. It isn't staying in one place. It is breaking into smaller ones. "Swiss-cheesing as they call it. It can go into the margins (I told you that yesterday). I learned today that if it goes into the margins it can go to other body parts.

Breast Cancer travels to one of three areas: lungs, bones, or liver. I will have an ultrasound in three weeks to see if it has gone into the margins and how small it is. Please pray it doesn't go into the margins.

I do believe God is healing me now (look at how good I look and feel)! And I am standing on His Word. I believe there will be a joyful ending and this Cancer will not be wasted. Somehow God will show me how I can get involved with other women who have it. Sharon, one of my nurses, told me that many women come in without any support system... how very sad.

I start round #2 on October 28th. It will be a shorter time in the lab - an hour more or less (smiling). I chose the drug Taxotere. Every three weeks for twelve weeks. As you know my last round of this is on September 30th.

I had a lovely chat with my nurse, Sharon. She is a strong Christian and said the majority of nurses in the lab are also. We talked about Bible studies we have both done, churches, version of Bibles. She looked at my Bible and said that it was surely loved and used as it is taped on both front and back covers.

One time, a friend saw it and said I should get it rebound. I said, "No way! What would I use while it's gone? I know where everything is." I do have other Bibles but they aren't the same. Many notes from three pastors in the margins.

Please pray for the woman next to me today. Her name is JoLynn. I'm not sure if she is a Christian, so throw in salvation, too. She is taking double the amount that I am on. This is her last session of her own round #1. Like me, JoLynn will be taking Taxotere for round #2. She has Breast Cancer. She did just the opposite as I am doing. I had chemo and will have surgery. She chose to have the lump removed and not the whole breast. The Cancer is also in her liver (not sure if it is from the Breast Cancer or just Liver Cancer on its own). JoLynn will know more in December to see if she can get on with her life or if she only has months to live. She said she is willing to wait as there is hope until December. Please add her to your prayer list.

On a lighter side, I am sleeping with a little soft hat on since my head gets chilly. How do you guys do it????

"God is our refuge and strength, a very pleasant help in trouble." (Psalm 46:1)

"There are two ways of getting out of a trial. One is to simply try to get rid of the trial and be thankful when it is over. The other way is to recognize the trial as a challenge from God to claim a larger blessing than we have ever had, and to hail it with delight as an opportunity of obtaining a larger measure of divine grace. Surely this is to be more than conquerors through HIM who loved us." (From Streams in the Desert, page 269).

I am choosing to smile, laugh, and not slow down... I am living my life! This is a challenge from God and I am embracing the entire journey. I am learning the depth of God's love for me and the trust I am gaining in His Sovereignty. Thus this journey has been and will continue to be worth it.

Love you all!

T.

P.S. I am off to a hot bath, bed, and a cup of green tea.

Outgoing email:
September 17th

Yesterday I found out that once in the margins, Cancer can move into the bones, liver, and lungs. However I am standing on Isaiah 41:10: *"God gave me in the beginning - You O Lord do not lie. Your promises are for your children."* And then in Jesus Calling it said, *'You will not find My peace by engaging in excessive planning; attempting to control what will happen to you in the future. I did not design the human mind to figure out the future. That is beyond your capability. I crafted your mind for continual commutation with Me. Bring me all your needs, your hopes and fears. Commit everything into My care. Turn from the path of planning to the path of peace.'"* (Jesus Calling, based on 1 Peter 5:6-7; Proverbs 16:9; Psalms 37:15, page 272)

Thank you Jesus, that my future is secure in your hands.

"Trust Me and refuse to worry, for I am your Strength and Song. You are feeling wobbly this morning looking at difficult times looming ahead, measuring them against your own strength Since I am your Strength I can empower you to handle each task as it comes. Because I am your Song, I can give you joy as you work alongside me..." (Jesus Calling, based on Exodus 15:2; 2 Corinthians 10:5; Hebrews 10:2, page 277)

O Abba Father, thank you that You are my strength and Song and You have the best for me and even in difficult times your thoughts towards me are for good and are more than the sands by the seas. When the winds blow hard and the boat is close to turning over, You will guide me into the shelter of You the Rock and in the towering cliff that is You where there is rest and safety.

I see John in Dr. Hoyer's office Tuesday. Chemo #4 is on Friday the 30th

Praying for you all,

T.

From my Prayer Journal
September 18th

Thank you for holding my hand Abba Father on the journey you and I are on. I am grateful for the trust I am learning - Your hand is on my head as a sheep walking next to her shepherd. I don't know the road we are on but you do. You have gone before me. I think of the verse you gave me, Isaiah 41:10. You will never leave me. Thank you for Your healing hand and there will be a joyful ending that the Cancer will gone. I must do it all - chemo, surgery, and radiation so I can help others somehow, digging wells in Bacca Valley. (Psalm 84:6)

The first prayer that Jason sent me from the Book of Common Prayer made me reflect:

My heart is filling with Your love - a love I never understood until now and even now I see only a glimmer of it. Now with calm expectancy I may make room for Your power to possess me and gracefully accept Your healing. Thank you. I take Your hand as the day begins.

Email outbox: September 22nd

Good Morning:

I am sharing with you the following as some of you may need encouragement as I did/do. The past few days the enemy has come with me with thoughts of death and dying due to my thinking of the Cancer going into the margins and thus a possibility of traveling to other body areas. This morning however, the battle started to turn to victory for me in my thinking.

"I call as my heart grows faint; lead me to the rock that is higher than I. When billow after billow rolls over us, and we are like a broken shell hurled to and from by the surf, Blessed be God that, at these times, we are not without an all-sufficient solace. Our God is the harbor of weather-beaten sails... Our God is a Rock because He does not change and a high Rock because the tempests which overwhelm us roll far beneath His feet; He is not disturbed by them, but rules them at His will. If we get under the shelter of this lofty Rock we may defy the hurricane; all is calm under the protection of that towering cliff." (Spurgeon's Morning and Evening, page 533)

"Trust Me and refuse to worry, for I am your Strength and Song. You are feeling wobbly this morning looking at difficult times looming ahead, measuring them against your own strength. Since I am your Strength I can empower you to handle each task as it comes. Because I am your Song I can give you joy as you work alongside me..." (From Jesus

Calling, based on Exodus 15:2; Corinthians 10:5; Hebrews 10:23, page 277)

O Abba Father, Thank you that You are my Strength and Song and you have the best for me and even in difficult times your thoughts towards me are for good and are more than the sands of the seas. When the winds blow hard and the boat is close to turning over You will guide me to the shelter of You the Rock, and in the towering cliff that is You where there is rest and safety.

I see John in Dr. Hoyer's office Tuesday and chemo #3 on Friday the 30th.

Praying for you all,

T.

Email inbox: from Deena Stuart
September 22nd

Praying for you too, dear Terry, I understand the wave of fear and I am praying against it - certainly Satan, whose desire is to unsettle you and push you into the crevice of fear. God is our great shield and the hiding place. Crawl into His lap - see yourself get up there-and be safe in His everlasting arms. He will see you through.

Email inbox: from Ed Altman

I thought you might like two poems in one of my Bible study books that I find helpful to me.

"When long and steep the path appears,
Or heavy is the Task,
OUR FATHER says, 'Press on, My child;
One step is all I ask.'" - D De Haan

"When serving the Lord and you lose your way,
Just hold out your hand and let JESUS lead;
He'll come to your aid, and you'll hear him say,
'I'll show you the way and meet every need'." - Hess

I hope you find these helpful to you during your ordeal.

Your friend
Ed Altman

From my Prayer Journal
September 22nd

"The LORD is my strength and song, and He has become
my salvation; this is my God, and I will praise Him; My
father's God and I will extol Him." Exodus 15:2.

Oh Jesus, I sit quietly in the early morning as the stars are
fading to hear you. Speak to me. I lay my requests of
continued healing for me - the Cancer not in the margins as
I hear you speak words of love, life, peace to me. I am
grateful I am your child. I wait as a child on Christmas Eve
to unwrap her presents. Please speak to those praying for
me.

September 25th
Email inbox: from Ed Altman

With HANDS on each other we asked Jesus to remove your Cancer problem. Hopefully you felt a surge of energy about 10am today as we prayed for TERRY! We went on to quote Ephesians 2:8 *"For it is by grace you have saved, through faith."* Also, our pastor quoted Psalm 91:14; *"Because he loves me says the Lord, I will him. I will rescue him. I will protect him, for he acknowledges my name. He will be with him in trouble. I will deliver him and honor him. With long life will I satisfy him, and show him MY salvation."* He also quoted Psalm 121 in its entirety, repeating 121:7: *"The Lord will keep you from all harm - He will watch over your life."*

Email outbox: September 28th

Good Morning:

Chemo #4 is tomorrow, Friday at 9:30. This is the last one for this round. I will then have three weeks off. During this time I will have an ultrasound to see how much of the Cancer is gone and where it is. Praying that it hasn't gone into the margins. It has gotten smaller but is now in several pieces. I will let you know the date when I know it.

They say that eating habits change with chemo. That is true. For those who know me, don't fall of the chair with the next line. I am eating meat. I know it is shocking and more shocking is that it tastes good. I told that to John today in Dr. Hoyer's office and he said I may be lacking in iron and with the blood they took today for chemo on Friday, he would have them do an iron panel. He called after reading the panel and my blood is really good. He said to eat what I like and to keep my weight stable, which it is. I love salads (not now) and fish is great, but beef is good. Go figure.

The last Friday in October I start round #2 of chemo with the drug (poison) Taxotere. It will be every three weeks for twelve weeks. This is one where there can be numbness in the hands and feet and nails can change color and/or fall off. Please pray that in this round there will no side effects, Thank you.

I will email you in October to keep you informed and so you won't forget to pray for me. Oh, I could never do any of this with a smile on my face without your prayers. Thank you!

"And they follow me" (John 10:27)

"We should follow our Lord as unhesitatingly as sheep follow their shepherd, for he has the right to lead us wherever he pleases. We are not our own. We are bought with a price – let's recognize the rights of the redeeming blood. Wherever Jesus may lead us, He goes before us. If we don't know where we are going, we know with whom we go. With such a companion, who will dread the perils of the road? All the ways of the Lord are loving and faithful for those who keep the demands of His covenant. Let's put full trust in our Leader, since we know that, come prosperity or adversity, sickness or health, popularity or contempt, His purpose shall be worked out, and that purpose shall be pure, unmingled good to every heir of mercy. We shall find

it sweet to go up the bleak side of the hill with Christ; and when rain and snow blow into our faces, His dear love will make us far more blessed than those who sit at home and warm their hands at the world's fire." (From Morning and Evening by Charles H. Spurgeon, page 525)

I know you too have a road to travel with Jesus. Thank you for taking time to travel my road of Cancer with prayer as you travel your individual road.

This morning as I was walking Annie, I prayed for those of you who are pastors that the Lord would give you wisdom as you prepare for Sunday Morning.

And for those of you who work in offices or businesses, that you would be good witnesses for Him to those you work with.

For those who sing, that your voices and harmonies would reach to heaven and God would smile.

For those who are parents, that you would listen to the voice of the Lord so your children would be more and more like Him.

For those of you in the arts, that your work would show the Creator.

For those of you who are grandparents, that the love you have for Jesus your grandchildren would see.

Have a great day with Jesus. I will let you know how Friday goes... please pray there will be nothing;

"Not even a ripple in the pond."

Love you all

T.

CHAPTER 4 – OCTOBER

Good Afternoon:

Tuesday is the ultrasound to see where the Cancer is and how much is gone. Praying none is in the margins! As I have thought about this, I realize the Cancer could be in the margins and then what? The following is what I wrote in my Prayer Journal and I would like to share it with you.

"But God you are sovereign and know what is best for me. I trust you. You are faithful and will not leave me. I have nothing to be anxious about. You will help me." (Isaiah 41:10)

If for some reason you allow the Cancer into the margins I will still praise you. *"For I found the one my heart loves. I held him and would not let him go."* (Song of Songs 3:4)

"My heart has made a covenant never to depart Him. O Lord I am grateful you have ratified it, as I want to dwell in beauty." (Phil. 4:6-8)

"The sparrow has made her nest for herself where she lay her young, even Your alter, O lord of Hosts, King and my God and so too would I make my nest, my home in You and never may the soul of Your turtle dove go forth from You

again, but may I nestle close to You, O Jesus, my true and only rest." (From Morning and Evening by Charles H. Spurgeon, page 547)

For thou has been a refuge for me. A tower of strength against the enemy. Let me dwell in Thy tent forever. Let me take refuge in the shelter of Thy wings." (Palms 61:3-4)

On a much lighter note: no more beef for me! My stomach has been somewhat nauseous the past few days. I think it is the beef and the chemo timing! I haven't eaten beef in years and to "load up" on it was silly on my part. No, it was dumb. I am going back to fish and salads.

Thank you for praying for the ultrasound.

Philemon 1:4-5

T.

October 3rd
Email inbox: from Jason

We are praying for you and will be tomorrow as you go in for the ultrasound.

"Heavenly Father, giver of life and health, comfort and relieve your servant Terry, and give your power of healing to those who minister to her needs, that she may be strengthened and have confidence and in your loving care through Jesus Christ or Lord.

Amen."

October 2nd
Email inbox: from Shari Brian

Lord Father,

You are wonderful. I love how Your thoughts are of peace and not of evil to give Terry a future and a hope! When You said in Your Word, *"Then you will call upon Me and go and pray to Me, and I will listen to you. And you will seek Me and find Me, when you search for Me with all your heart. I WILL BE FOUND BY YOU!"*

When You said, *"And I will bring you back from your captivity,"* You meant it! Each time the enemy thinks he's won a skirmish with Terry's Cancer, YOU counteract him with a WIN! He thinks she is held captive by a chemo pump, but as I watched her wait, I saw that it's not a chemo pump holding her captive - it's YOU holding her heart captive! Right in the midst of the enemy's best shot. You caused her to Live Your Word right there in that chemo room - comforting and encouraging those around her (me AND her pastor, not to mention the other patients) and amazing the nurses with her great faith.

So Satan has now reverted to the only thing he has left as a weapon – fear - and even that is only possible if he can get her to play "what-if". But Jesus, anoint her to play the "what-if" game your way. What-if.

"Your Word is TRUE - and it is!" (John 7:28; Romans 3:4; Philippians 4:8; Revelation 21:5)

"What-if you heal just as Your Word declares - and you Do! "(Psalm 103:3-4; Luke 4:18)

When the enemy comes in like a flood, talk to her Jesus, sing over her, whisper secrets of the Most High that make her thoughts captive to the TRUTH of Psalms 91:15! I pray that You will answer her every prayer, anoint her to focus her thoughts on you (on purpose) - and restore to her great peace and assurance in this entire process.

In Jesus' name.

Amen.

Email outbox: October 4th

Good Afternoon:

If I could have a drink of champagne I would! But will have to wait until January when chemo is done. The ultrasound was good... No, it was GREAT! The Cancer is shrinking. It is now a 2 and it was 3.5. The lumpy stuff in the breast in me is also a thick wall that my body is building to contain the Cancer. That is how my body is fighting the Cancer. Pretty cool huh?!!

The radiologist felt the left side and it is lumpy... she did an ultrasound on it as well to give peace of mind... all is ok and clean. She said I was complicated and a hard case due to the lumpiness. I told her that is what I have been told before... before the Cancer. She laughed. She said I am on target and to keep doing what I have been doing. As she walked out with me I told her I was a Christian and that

God was doing amazing work in me and that as hard as this has been I wouldn't trade it for anything.

She looked at me strangely and said, "So you are learning a lot?"
I said, "Oh yes... more than I ever knew I could learn from and about the LORD and I am not even have half way done."
I told her when in chemo I am having quiet moments, smiling, reading my Bible. When friends stop by we talk and laugh while others nearby seem so sad and alone. I want to help somehow. She said she would be praying about that.

I want to share with you what I wrote in my Prayer Journal.

"Help me, O LORD my God; save me according to Thy loving kindness. And let them know that this is thy hand, Thou, LORD has done it." (Psalm 109:26-27)

"I shall not die, but live and tell of the works of the LORD." Psalm 118:17 (I do want to write a book about this journey.)

You O LORD are mighty to save! Thank you that you did and have stopped the Cancer, that you have allowed my body to build walls around the Cancer to contain it.

I think of Psalm 34:7 *"The angel of the Lord encamps around those who fear Him and rescues them."*

Oh, Abba Father, the Great I Am, you are more than the sum of your parts - just look at your names and their meaning.

And all creation, even the rocks would cry out to you if your children didn't offer praise to you...

From the vast jungles to the tiny snow-capped flowers on high mountains;

To the oceans of water to the oceans of sand;

To the animals from the tiny frogs and bees to the roaring lions and long necked giraffe in Africa;

To the elk and bears in North America...

Yes, you are an amazing God... more than the whole. I have been praying when I walk Annie in the early morning that the Lord would give an equally stronger, deeper more profound walk like He is doing with me.

Psalm 1:1-3

T.

Email outbox: October 10th

Good Morning:

"In me - peace." (John 16:33)

There is a vast difference between happiness and blessedness. Paul's imprisonments and pains, sacrifice and suffering up to the very limit; but in the midst of it all, he was blessed. All the beatitudes came into his heart and life in the midst of those very conditions.

I am reminded of an old story:

Paganini, the great violinist, came out before his audience one day and made the discovery just as they ended their applause that there was something wrong with his violin. He looked at it a second time and saw that it was not his famous valuable one. He felt paralyzed for a moment. He turned to his audience and told them there must have been some mistake and that he did not have his own violin.

He stepped back behind the curtain thinking that it was still where he had left it, but discovered that someone had stolen his and left an old secondhand one on in its place. Paganini remained back behind the curtain for a moment, then came out before his audience and said, "Ladies and Gentlemen, I will show you that the music is not in the instrument, but in the soul."

He played as he had never played before, and out of that secondhand instrument, the music poured forth until the audience was enraptured with enthusiasm and the applause almost lifted the ceiling of the building, because the man had revealed to them that music was not in the machine but in his own soul.

It is your mission, a tested and tried one, to walk out on the stage of this world and reveal to all earth and heaven that the music is not in the condition, not in the things, not in externals, but in the music of life is in your soul." (From Streams in the Desert, pgs. 288-289)

"Be silent unto God and let Him mold thee." (Psalm 46:10)

"'Rest pause' contribute to the finer music of life." (From Springs in the Valley, page 242)

"Thank you for praying for me. I pray for you that the LORD will bring out the symphony that is each of you for His Glory." Philippines 4:19

T.

**From my Prayer Journal
October 11th**

Philippians 4:8 says, *"Finally brethren, whatever is true, whatever is honorable, whatever is right, whatever is pure, whatever is lovely, whatever is of good repute, if there is any excellence and if anything worthy of praise, let your mind dwell on these things."*

I have written in the margin of my Bible, "The above is Jesus". My goal continues to be to keep my eyes on Him. But in the world of daily life I am choosing to dwell in what is lovely:

The music of a symphony

A walk in a meadow of wild flowers

The laughter of children

Emerson

The quiet of the early morning with Jesus

The sound of rain

A rainbow in the sky

The smell of lavender and lilacs

Horses in a pasture grazing in the sun

Annie sleeping with her nose in an open window in the sunroom

October 12th
Email inbox: from Joy Lundy

I have been thinking about you, as we are studying Acts in our Bible study and how through the persecutions and scattering of the disciples the Word of God was spread to all people. You too, are spreading His Word through tough times.

Email outbox: October 13th

Good Afternoon:

I saw Sherry, Dr. Hoyer's nurse this afternoon to get ready for round 2 of chemo. It starts October 28 at 9:30. The drug is Taxotere. The side effects can be: low white and red blood cells counts. Fluid retention that can last a few days at the beginning. Numbness in fingers and toes. This may occur more towards the end with repeated doses.

Other possibilities:

Hair loss

Nausea

Diarrhea

Mouth sores

Bone pain

Liver problems

Fatigue

Weakness

Nail changes (color and falling off).

They have found that when the Taxotere is going in, if my nails or both hands and feet are in ice (for about an hour), then the color and falling off won't happen or will be less. Skin and or eyes can also turn yellow

While the Taxotere is going in there could be allergic reactions (rash, fever, and low blood pressure) and like the last round I need to be careful of cuts and bruises due to bleeding. Thank you for praying NO side effects like the last chemo. The upside is my last treatment is December 30th. HAPPY NEW YEARS!

I have chemo every 3 weeks: October 28th. November 18th. December 9th. December 30th.

Like before, I have the shot on Saturdays to help keep the white blood cell count good.

"And whatever you ask in My name, that will I do, that the Father may be glorified in the Son if you ask Me anything in My name, I will do it." (John 14:13-14)

"Think a moment who it is that promises: The God who holds the sea in the hollow of His hand; the God who swings this ponderous globe of earth in its orbit; the God who marshals the stars and guides the planets in their blazing paths with undeviating accuracy; the heaven-creating, devil-conquering, dead-raising God. It is this very God who says; 'If ye ask I will do.' Unrivaled wisdom, boundless skill, limitless power, infinite resources are His." (Springs in the Valley, pgs. 295, 296)

Thank you for your prayers as I continue down this road with round 2. I will be praying God will do Marvels in your life like He has done and will continue to do in mine.

Ephesians: 6:24

T.

October 13th
Email inbox: from Bonnie McGowan

This was a hard one to read. The side effects possible for your next round. I'm definitely praying for you, Terry – specifically no side effects. And know that God hasn't left you and He never will. He'll walk every inch with you and

I'm so thankful for that. I'll walk every inch of this with you in prayer. God bless you and give you a good night's sleep tonight.

October 16th
From my Prayer Journal

Thank you, Jesus. I can look to you for continual help, comfort and companionship because you are always at my side. You enfold me in your arms. Thank you that you're with me in this pièce de résistance: the summit of salvation blessing. No matter what losses I experience no one can take this away from me. (Based on Psalm 34: 4-6, Psalm 105: 4, 2 Corinthians 1: 3-4 from Jesus Calling, page 303)

When I need comfort, you enfold me in your arms like Jason does for Emerson, the peace, gentleness and quietness of a parent's love. I am thankful that others see you in me on this road we are walking together called Cancer.

"Let us lay aside every weight that encumbers us, the sin which so easily entangles us, and let us run with endurance the race that is set before us," (Hebrews 12:1)

The failure of Israel to enter the land of promise began in murmuring or, as the text in Numbers literally puts it, "as it were murmured". Just a faint desire to complain and be discontented that blossomed and ripened into rebellion and ruin.

Oh Jesus, help me never to be like that again, but to always remember your faithfulness walking with me.

The devil uses his tricks of discouragement and doubt. To stand against these I must have a heart full of gladness and joy in the Holy Spirit and always remember Isaiah 41:10, the verse You gave me. Thank you. (Based on Streams in the Desert)

SECOND PHASE OF CHEMO BEGINS...

Email outbox: October 19th

Good morning:

Thank you for praying for me. It seems not enough to say that simple phase.

"By reason of breaking they purify themselves." (Job 41:25)

"God uses most for His glory those people and things which are most perfectly broken. The sacrifices He accepts are broken and contrite heart..." (Psalm 51:17)

"Jacob at Peniel (Genesis 32: 25-32); Moses when he broke the surface rock at Horeb to get water (Exodus 17:6) Gideon and 300 elect soldiers who broke the pitchers to see the hidden lights (Judges 7:16-22); Esther risked her life and broke through the rigid etiquette of a heathen count to save her people from death (Esther 4:14-17); Jesus breaking the five loaves and feeding the five thousand (Matthew 14: 17-20); Mary breaking her alabaster box and the perfume filled the room as it ran down over Jesus' head (Mark 14:3); Jesus allowing His precious body to be broken to pieces by thorns and nails for our sins (John 19:1-30).

God must have broken things. Those who are broken in wealth, and broken in self-will, and broken in their ambitions, and broken in their beautiful ideals, and broken in wordily reputation and broken in their affections, and broken ofttimes in their health, those who are despised and seem utterly forlorn and helpless, the Holy Spirit is seizing upon, and using for God's glory. 'The lame take the prey.'"
(Isaiah 33:23, from Streams in the Desert page 305)

O Lord, how exciting to be on this Cancer journey with you. The road that was handpicked by You to refine me as gold. I pray each day and each turn in the road I will look to see you there and not fear. I will be a sheep wagging its tail waking next to its Shepherd as we continue to travel on these next few months together.

I would like to remind my prayer warriors that Friday the 28th starts round two of chemo. Thank you for praying for no side effects. This morning I read in Daniel 3 about the three men in the fire. I want my testimony to be of God's faithfulness and greatness. I too, want to be out of this fire of Cancer with no smell of fire or singed hair or scorched clothes. I sense from the Lord that as I pray for you, you are my mission field. Some have to travel the world to have a mission field but I get one by praying for you. Now that is exciting. Isn't it?

Psalm 119:105

T.

From my Prayer Journal
October 24th

Round two of chemo starts this Friday the 28th. Thank you thus far that there have been no side-effects. I pray there won't be any with this round. Help me to unwind in your presence as my shepherd to lie down in green pastures and enjoy time with You. Thank you that You have called to walk down paths of peace with you - that this Cancer journey was needed for me to see the need to walk with a gentler step and enjoy life. Thank you too for choosing me with my weaknesses and not any strengths I might have.

Your grace is sufficient. This shows my need for you all the time on His road I am walking with you as well as other areas of my life. I pray others will see you in me and long to know you better. Please take away all anxious thoughts that come to mind as I wait for Friday. You know best. Thank you for healing me completely - that the Cancer will be no more ever again in me! (Based on Jesus Calling, page 311, based on Genesis 2: 2-3, Luke 1:79)

Email outbox: October 26th

Good Morning:

This Friday, in two days, starts round two of chemo... It should take an hour or a little more with one poison, not two like before.

"For He commands and raises the stormy wind, which lifts up the waves of the sea." (Psalm 107:25)

"Stormy winds fulfilling His word. By the time wind blows upon us it is His word for us. God's winds do effectual work. They shake loose from us the things that can be shaken, that those things which cannot be shaken may remain, those eternal things which belong to the Kingdom which cannot be moved. They have their part to play in stripping us and strengthening us so that we may be more ready for the uses of Eternal Love. Then can we refuse to welcome?

Be like the pine on the hilltop, Alone with God.

There is a curious comfort in remembering that the Father depends upon His child not to give way. It is inspiring to be trusted with a hard thing. You never asked for summer breezes to blow upon your tree. It is enough that you are not alone upon the hill. And let the storm that does Thy work deal with me as it may." (From Springs in the Valley, pgs. 299, 300)

Dear Lord, in two days starts round two of chemo. I am asking once again for no side effects. Thank you for being on the hilltop with me as your wind comes. Let the wind hit me in the face for all is well. You are with me and will not forsake me. Your love is everlasting. I agree with Augustus Toplady (who also wrote Rock of Ages) when he said, *"Nothing in my hand I bring, simply to thy cross I cling."*

Praying for you.

T.

Email outbox: October 28th

Good Morning:

I just finished my quiet time with the LORD and I would like to share some thoughts with you.

"Therefore encourage one another, and build up one another, just as you also are doing. But we request of you brethren that you appreciate those who diligently labor among you and have charge over you in the LORD and give you instruction." (I Thessalonians 5:11-12)

Thank you for your prayers, emails of prayers, encouragement, smiles and chats at church and work when I see some of you. Laughter in pottery class, phone calls, chats and pats on the backs and lots of smiles and laughter in the doctor's office and chemo lab. I feel like Gene Kelly in his now famous song and dance when he twirled his umbrella splashing in the rain puddles in the movie *Singing in the Rain.*

I feel great peace and I too, am dancing in the rain, splashing in the rain with Jesus as I face today. There is a painting I have seen (should have bought it) of a lone sheep standing on a hill among rolling hills in Ireland. That was all that was in the painting. I am reminded that I am that sheep looking at The Lord for my directions for the day.

As your sheep standing on the hill looking for directions for today, I want others to see you in me in the chemo lab. Thank you in advance for no side effects. Thank you for those praying for me. Bless them, protect them, let them fly with the eagles in the air currents with you. I open my hand to hold yours as this day begins."

Off to walk Annie and pray for you. Thanks for standing with me. Your prayers are why I am doing so well. I don't understand how or why the Creator of the Universe, the Great I Am, works though His children's prayers for HIs Glory. He does and I am grateful and humbled by it all. Love you all,

T.

Email outbox: October 28th

Good Afternoon:

God is So amazing! So far No side effects! There were two pre-drips. The second one was Benadryl. I told my nurse I could have reactions to it. She said she would watch me. I was fine. Then when the Taxotere started she did it three times slower, and then moved it faster about every fifteen minutes. By the fourth time I was up to full speed. She watched me very closely and again no side effect. This took about ninety minutes.

While the Taxotere was going in the port my toes and the tips of my fingers were in ice bags. It helped, as I had very little pain due to numbness. My nails did not change color or start falling off.

I am reading *The Westminster Confession of Faith*. It is nice to pull my fingers out of the ice and turn the pages. The Day-After-shot is tomorrow at 1pm.

The next chemo sessions are scheduled for November 18th and 19th. It was a good morning as I danced with my umbrella in the rain with Jesus. What an adventure this is! Who would have thought Cancer would do this to me?

Answer: God.

Thank you for your faithful prayers. I will email you during the next two weeks.

Hebrews 13:25

T.

October 28th
Email inbox: from Zetta Henson

YAH!!! God is good! And I'm so grateful that He has put you in my life, Terry! I'm a better person because of you and your story. Thank you for being my friend and loving me, You are certainly loved - By ME!

Email outbox: October 28th

Good Evening:

One last email in reference to the chemo lab today. As I sat with the drip going in, one of the volunteers sat by my side to give words of encouragement and chat. She was there during the first chemo round. I saw her a lot then. It was fun to chat this time around. When she saw me today she smiled and asked how I was doing.

I told her "fine".

She then said, "So the battle is going well?"

I said, "I hate buzz words - battle, survivor - to name two. This isn't a battle. I may be naive and looking at this too simply, but I see it no differently than a broken leg. God heals broken legs and He heals Cancer. I am not in the middle of the ocean treading water battling sharks and the elements."

She responded with a strange look and said, "I have never heard anyone say that before. When I had Cancer, every morning I would get up, look at myself in the mirror and say, 'the battle has begun'."

I said, "Wasn't that exhausting? My whole life I have been fighting battles of one kind or another. Sometimes I think I am Don Quixote always fighting windmills. But I have no control over this. I am being obedient to my doctors and trusting God. It is rather refreshing and peaceful to watch God do what he wants in my life. I have no decisions to make nor worry if I made the right decision."

She smiled and said, "Talking with you is always so uplifting,"

I told her she too was encouraging to me.

She ended the conversation with, "Isn't it nice to know that God deals with all of us differently."

I said, "Yes," and that, "he didn't want a bunch of robots. He treats us as individuals. That is why there is free will," I told her. "I am amazed the many times I blow it and He is still there pointing the way and holding my hand."

She agreed.

Have a great weekend with Jesus

Psalm 139:7-12

T.

October 30th
Email inbox: from Ruth Mott

I prayed for you regarding this round of chemo. I am blessed to hear that there have been no side effects. I have not been able to read my emails for two days and had several from you. I chose this one to reply to because your attitude toward all of this is so wonderful, godly, and inspirational (as shown through all your emails).

I know it is Jesus In you, giving forth His nature through you. As I read all your emails and the devotionals you send, I see the faith of Hebrews 4 (the believer's rest) and 11 (the triumph of faith) exhibited through you. I give God all the glory for sustaining you in such a beautiful way through you each and every day. He is your Lord, this is so obvious. What a Privilege to know and love you.

October 30th
From my Prayer Journal

Thank you, Lord for no side effects from Friday's chemo.

Psalm 104: 33-34.

I want to have as my daily life goal - to praise You - to sing to You as long as I live - praise from my soul - all of me. May my meditations be pleasing to You. I will be glad in you, Jesus my Rock! I know you are doing amazing things in me. You will never leave me.

Psalm 23:1-3 says: *"The LORD is my shepherd, I shall not want. He makes me lie down in green pastures; He leads me beside quiet waters. He restores my soul; He guides me in the paths of righteousness For His name sake."*

Round two of chemo starts Friday the 28th. Thank you. Thus far that there have been no side-effects. I pray there won't be any this round. I pray others will see you in me and long to know you better.

Please take away all anxious thoughts that come to mind as I wait for Friday. You know best. Thank you for healing me completely - that the Cancer will be no more, never again in me. I Trust you as you lead me in green pastures and quiet waters. I love you, Jesus.

I want to always be like the one leper you healed and he returned to give you thanks not like the nine who kept walking. (Luke 17: 12-18)

CHAPTER 5 – NOVEMBER

Email outbox: November 3rd

Good Afternoon:

Once again I would like to thank you for praying for me. The journey is half over for chemo. The surgery is scheduled for the end of January. Radiation in February.

Some thoughts from Charles H. Spurgeon's Morning and Evening:

"He is praying. (Acts 9:11) Prayers are instantly noticed in heaven. 'You list my tears on your scroll,' implies that they are recorded as they flow. The suppliant, whose fears prevent his words, will be understood by the Most High. Our God not only hears prayers but also loves to hear it. He doesn't regard the triumph and pride of man; but wherever there is a heart big with sorrow, or a lip quivering with agony, or a deep groan, or a penitential sigh, the ear of Jehovah is open; He marks it down in the registry of His Memory; Our prayers, like rose leaves, between the pages of His book of remembrance, and when the volume is opened at last, a precious fragrance will release itself from it." (Page 616)

"Their prayers reached Heaven, his holy dwelling place." (2 Chronicles 30:27)

"Prayer is the unfailing recourse of the Christian in any situation, in every plight. Your powder may be damp, your bowstring may be relaxed, but the weapon of all prayer needn't ever be out of order. Leviathan laughs at the javelin, but he trembles at prayers. In every condition whether of poverty, or sickness, or obscurity or slander, or doubt, your covenant God will welcome your prayer and answer it from His holy place. Nor is prayer ever futile. True prayer is always true power. YOU may not always get what you ask for, but you shall have your real wants supplied. When God does not answer His Children according to the letter, He does so according to the spirit. If you ask for coarse meal, will you get angry because He gives you the finest flour?" (page 617).

"I will praise you, O Lord". (Psalm 9:1)

"Praise should always follow answered prayer; as the mist of earth's gratitude rises when the sun of heaven's love warms the ground. Has the Lord been gracious to you, and inclined His ear to the voice of your supplication? Then Praise Him as long as you live. Don't deny singing to Him who has answered your prayer and given you the desire of your heart. To be silent over God's mercies is to incur the guilt of ingratitude; it is to act as basely as the nine lepers who, after they had been cured of their leprosy, never returned to give thanks to the healing of the Lord. Those who have been in similar circumstances will take comfort if we can say, 'Glory the Lord with me; let us exalt His name together; the poor man called and the LORD heard him.' The angels don't pray, but they never cease to praise both day and night; and the redeemed, clothed in white robes with palm branches in their hands, are never weary of singing the new song, 'Worthy is the Lamb.'"(page 608)

I know the above is long but it proves the importance of prayer not only for me but also whomever the Lord lays on your heart and that HE does hear and answer. I know sometimes it seems like years but He is faithful in His timing and answer. I want to be like the lone leper who returns with praise and singing to God for what He had done in his life. I want to be like that leper for what He has done in my life and yours. Won't you offer up praise to God with me?

Psalm 104:33

T.

Email outbox: November 6th

Good Afternoon:

This past week was hard. What started as a cold (or so I thought) turned into the flu by the weekend. There were several times I wanted to have a pity party. But I knew I couldn't as there are so many people who have it far worse than I do from Cancers that are killing, to no health insurance.

I remembered the old Nike advertisement: "Never let them see you sweat."

I was told, "I can't believe you don't have any side effects."

I responded with, "I asked for prayer with no side effects and God answers and works through our prayers."

I don't know why He chose to say "yes" to me and "no" to others. I then had a rather large guilt party for a little while. I thought maybe if I was nauseous and didn't want to eat and my nails were falling out and I had no insurance, then I would be ok to ask for prayer. I know better than anyone that God is showing HUGE Grace and Mercy towards me. I know I am a sinner saved by His death on the cross and he chose me from before the foundations of the world to be His child.

I have asked "why"? I think He has a gentle voice and hand to draw me back. I also believe I can't lose my salvation. This past week I was just "going through the motions" of my early morning quiet time with the Lord. I think this Cancer road is something God has picked for me to see just how much I can/would trust Him.

I lost the focus for a short time but it is back now! But God, (don't you love that phrase) this morning the sun came out and I could see the light at the end of the tunnel both physically and mentally.

"God also hath sent the one (thing) over against the other." Ecclesiastes 7:14

"Too often we see life's prose, but not the poetry. Too often we miss the inspiration of the songs. How manifold are your sorrow, but how manifold are His gifts! Sin is here, but so is boundless grace; the devil is here, but so is Christ; the sword of judgment is crossed by Mercy's scepter. God never strikes the wrong note; never sings the wrong song. If God makes music, the music will prove medicinal... listen for the night songs of God!" (From Springs in the Valley, pgs 319-320)

Psalm 104: 33-34 says, *"I will sing to the LORD as long as I live; I will sing praise to my God while I have my being. Let my meditations be pleasing to Him; as for me, I shall be glad in the LORD."*

I want to have as my daily goal to praise you in all circumstances. You, Jesus are my Rock. I know you are doing amazing things in me and though me. I want always to be like the leper you healed and he returned to give you thanks not like the nine who kept walking. (Luke 17:12-18)

I talked to my sister Leigh Ann this week. She called to see how I was doing. She shared what her pastor had talked about. They were in Mark, Chapter 4:35-41, where Jesus told his disciples to get into the boat and they would go to the other side. A fierce gale of wind came up on them and the disciples were afraid. Jesus was sleeping in the boat. After he awoke and rebuked the wind and the sea, he made a very simple statement. *"Remember who is in the boat with you."*

I have hung on to that for a few days with a smile. So after a week of physically not feeling well and mentally fighting imaginary windmills, I am back to my old feisty self. "Back in the saddle again," as the saying goes. Jesus has popped my fears and worries like popping a balloon. I am once again walking down the road with Him with a skip in my step and a smile on my face – ah, life is good.

Next chemo is the 18th at 9 AM. With the flu I haven't really eaten like I should. I am down to 120 pounds and need to gain at least three more by the 18th. Yesterday and today I have had my glass of "pond scum" green stuff and will fix something lovely for dinner. Thank you for your prayers.

Psalm 44: 4, 5

T.

November 9th
Email inbox from Phyllis Jordahl

What a great testimony email; you have a great book to write. We are so pleased you are doing better, now we pray you gain weight. I pray for you often in the night when I wake up.

Email inbox from Jan Allums

May we never cease to pray for you! Like David you never quit until you work through to Him.

Email inbox from Bonnie McGowan

It was good to get your note. You came through the "Red Sea". Darkness in the back of you and dry land and sunshine in front of you. Only God can do that and I'm so thankful we have him.

Corrie Ten Boom, while she was imprisoned, constantly remembered that we are "In Christ, in God." She would take her thumb (represents Corrie), place it in the palm of her hand (same hand... represents her in Christ), and take the other four fingers of her hand (same hand) and wrap them tightly over her thumb (represents Corrie, in Christ, in God).

Hope this makes sense. I do it all the time - just knowing that He's holding me. I continue to pray for you Terry, especially as you approach the 18th. May God be your strength in time of weakness and your resting place of peace."

Email outbox: November 15th

Good Afternoon:

This is long so get comfy, a cup of tea.

One of my favorite books is F.LaGard Smith's Meeting God in Quiet Places - The Cotswold Parables. The following refers to chapter 24 of Five Black Cows, page 220, 221).

"My comfort in my suffering is this: Your promise renews my life." (Psalm 119:50).

The author, Mr. Smith, had hurt his knee and could barely walk. He gave it a rest for two days and then thought it might be good enough for a cautious workout. With his trusty walking stick he headed out into one of the narrow equestrian trails leading to the next village.

He was limping like an old man struggling one step after step until he reached a path that wound its way from one field to another where he climbed over a fence with the help of one of the ingeniously constructed stiles that are found on all walking paths in England.

Once over the fence he saw five very familiar faces - five cows. He had walked past these five black cows on many of his daily walks and they had never paid him the slightest bit of attention. They would usually keep munching grass as he passed them.

As F. LaGard Smith wrote: *"But this day was strangely different. They all stopped eating and looked curiously about his bent frame and slow gait. Then, to his great amazement they slowly began following him, in a single file, something they had never done before, as if to say, 'Let's walk with the old guy for a while.' He was lost in thought but then all of a sudden he saw them running toward him as if to say, "Enough of this limping stuff, let's run for a while!" They skidded to a halt and began playfully butting heads with each other."*

As he turned around and started to walk off, he realized he could walk again! Praise God, he was healed! He could tell the knee was working properly again. Did he pray as he was climbing over the fence? Would he have attributed the healing to a divine miracle and why not? He was thankful to God in any event. He knew God can bring healing. As in the Book of James, fervent prayer may well be the avenue which such a miracle of healing comes. But Jesus did not attempt to heal every suffering person during his ministry.

God's greater concern is about our spiritual health, and perhaps about how we might respond to having a broken body.

"Rather than being the cause of his healing out in the field he thought God was more like the five black cows. They weren't there to heal him that day, but seemed to sense something different in him and may well have decided to

'walk with the old guy for a while.' For him that is all he needed to know about the Great Physician.

Whether he heals me or not. I'll still give him all the praise. He knows better than I do what's best for me. It's enough simply to know that there is always Someone who will walk with me, no matter how badly my life is limping along.

As John Henry Jowett put it, 'God does not comfort us to make us comfortable, but to make us comforters.' When he thinks of ordinary people comforting others, he thought of Job's friends, Blidad and Zophar, who went 'to sympathize with him and comfort him'.

What do you say to the mourning couple who have just lost their child?

Or to the friend whose spouse has just walked away from the marriage?

What words can prove adequate for the person dying of Cancer or other deadly diseases?

How do you possibly answer the grief-stricken 'Why' that follows the fatal auto crash?

These earlier years he would attempt at comforting by somehow fixing the situation. Say the right words, call the right people, and quote the perfect Scripture to 'make everything right'.

Now he realizes the futility of trying to change the circumstances. Death, pain, sorrow, and the whole range of human suffering is a natural part of this world that won't just go away. If there is insight and wisdom to be shared or a word of Scripture that truly speaks to the situation at hand, then that can be a comfort. And joining together in prayer can itself be an act of compassion. But godly comfort need only join heart to heart in love. For comfort is not simply a matter of soothing or easing pain. The word 'comfort' literally means to 'make strong'. When hearts join with other hearts, there is strength to withstand what one heart alone could not endure. Nowadays he mostly sets in silence. It's the quiet hug, the tender touch that brings comfort. That which is already known need not be spoken.

Just our being there is what people need. To know we care. God's comfort does not always come in the form of healing. It doesn't always take away the pain or change the circumstances. But just knowing God is with us, whatever the circumstances, was enough for him.

He could have been wrong about the five black cows. What cow would ever think, 'Let's walk with the old guy for awhile'? But what a comforting thought: God sensing everything that impacts our lives, and walking along with us - no matter how slight the limp, no matter how serious the suffering."

Thank you for joining your hearts with mine on this journey, knowing your prayers are there and that you don't need to try and fix it or give words of wisdom, but like the five black cows you are here walking with me.

I had an appointment this morning with Wendy at Dr. Hoyer's office, a follow-up from the chemo on the 28th of October. She is concerned that the right breast is the same size so I am going to have another MRI within the next two weeks. It should be smaller. I asked her if I should be concerned and she said, "Not yet" (lovely).

I told her about having the flu and she said it could have been a side effect. Every seven to fourteen days is when something bad can happen (the bleeding that happened with round #1). She said if it happens again to call the office. She was a little upset with me that I didn't call this time. I honestly thought it was the flu. She said I still should have called. Chemo is this Friday the 18th at 9am.

Thank you for praying and walking with me. (You are a great black cow.)

T.

From my Prayer Journal
November 16th

Thank you for giving me my prayer warriors who like the five black cows in the book, *Quiet Times With God*, are walking with me - praying for me. Thank you Lord when this road we are on seems to get tangles of branches and limbs and I can't see. I must remember you are holding my hand and won't leave me. Thank you that you will lead the way - breaking the limbs and taking me one step at a time. I am asking that since I had the flu last week, that it will not affect the chemo this coming Friday. And please, that after the chemo on Friday the breast will get smaller. And no side effects.

Email outbox: November 18th

Good Afternoon:

Just got home from chemo #2. Went well. A little tired. Could be from the Benadryl (pre-chemo drip). Going to lay down for a bit...

Closing thought:

"Faith is a living, daring confidence in God's grace, so sure and certain that a man could stake his life on it a thousand times." (Martin Luther).

"Beware of squatting lazily before God instead of putting up a glorious fight that you may lay hold of His Strength." (Oswald Chambers)

Thank you for your faith in God's grace and for not "Squatting lazily before God". Thank you for praying for me! I am praying for you.

MRI on Tuesday November 29 at 11:30.

Psalm 26:11,12

T.

From my Prayer Journal
November 19th

Thank you!!! Chemo #2 went well yesterday and no side effects. Thank you that I can with total faith and trust leave the outcome to you. It is an adventure! I want to enjoy the rhythm of life living close to you. I already know my ultimate destination is living with you. I will keep my focus on the path - each step - and leave the outcome to you.

Email outbox: November 22nd

Happy Thanksgiving:

"Give thanks to the LORD, for He is good! Let the redeemed of the LORD say so." Psalm 107:1-2

The whole reason for saying thanks is to let the giver of the gift know how much you appreciate something. Author G.B. Stern once said, *"Silent gratitude isn't much use to anyone".* And William Arthur Ward said, *"Feeling gratitude and not expressing is it like wrapping a present and not giving it."* (From Daily Bread).

I would like to express my heartfelt gratitude for each of you in my life, some for a long time and some more recently, but each important! Your prayers mean the world to me and the emails and smiles when I see you are just icing on the cake. This Cancer journey would be next to impossible without you.

We have much to be thankful for this Thanksgiving. In spite of the evil, wars, rumors of wars, pain, hurt and confusion in the world, God is still in control. He is still on

His throne. The Maker of heaven and earth isn't shocked. We are held in the grip of His love, He knows what is best for us and His timing is perfect.

Happy Thanksgiving to each of you. I pray you will have a wonderful day with family and friends and know you are loved to the moon and back.

Psalm 28:7

T.

November 24th
From my Prayer Journal

Today is Thanksgiving. I have much to be thankful for. You are my God, healing me, my family (Jason, Tara, Emerson), my prayer warriors.

"There is nothing that separates me from your love. As I go through the day I shall look at tiny treasures placed by you to brighten my day. Oh what a lovely bouquet and then I shall give it to you." (From Jesus Calling, page 342, based on Psalm 4:7-8, Romans 8: 38-39)

November 27th
From my Prayer Journal

Pure nard, (a perfume for burials) very costly (John 12:3).

"Possibly it was only an impulse which made Mary decide to anoint Jesus beforehand. One tiny violet of encouragement will mean more to those with whom we live today than will acres of orchids when their pules are stilled to death. There is no fragrance like that of my alabaster box - the box I break for Him!" (From Springs in the Valley, page 337)

Jesus I want most of all for you to see the love I have for you - this Cancer road you choose for me for that very purpose - all these years of doubts and fears and holding back. I see now your amazing love for me.

I love you Jesus.

Email outbox: November 29th

Good Morning:

Sunday in church, Pastor Mark Bates started the Advent season off with a message called: *Christmas; the Unfolding Promise.* He used Matthew 1:1-17 as his base. How it is important that the genealogy of Jesus Christ shows that he is the son of David. That shows that Jesus has rights to His kingdom and He is sitting now at the Right hand of God the Father. He is ruling and will return to rule earth as well.
And he is the son of Abraham showing he is the son of the covenant promise keeping God. Matthew named four women who were in Jesus' genealogy, not ones who were

"good and noble, etc". But he chose these four who had a questionable past at best.

And the fact that women are named at all is amazing for at the time women didn't have a lot of value until Jesus came. Jesus came for the needy and weak. When you read who these four women are in the Bible they were needy and weak, too. Tamar (Genesis 38); Bathsheba (2 Samuel 12:24) ; Ruth (Ruth 4:17:22) and Rehab (Matthew 1:5)

I find that so very encouraging; for I too am needy and weak. God is accomplishing His purpose and keeps His promises. I have two more chemo's the 9th of December and the 30th of December. This phase of chemo has gone fast and I am so grateful there are no side effects except for being tired, always cold and bleeding during the seven to ten days because I am not careful.

I have nothing to complain about and yet I know I am needy and weak without your prayers. My growing trust and faith in God's love for me is wider, longer, higher, and deeper than anything I have ever known. I am learning to release into His care anything that could be a concern and to be thankful for everything He brings my way regardless of how small.

God is accomplishing beautiful and wonderful things with His purposes in my life and He is keeping His promises. I just know at the end of March when everything is over: chemo, surgery, radiation... I will be healed and well and on a much closer walk with Him than I ever knew could be.

If He is doing beautiful and wonderful things in my life, He is in yours as well, because of Christmas the unfolding Promise.

Closing thought:

"We have to realize that we cannot learn or win anything from God; we must either receive it as a gift or do without." Oswald Chambers.

Isaiah 49:16

T.

CHAPTER 6 - DECEMBER

Email outbox: December 6th

Good Evening:

This one will take a cup of tea or two...a bit long.

"Along unfamiliar paths I will guide them." (Isaiah 42:16)

(Again, from Meeting God in Quiet Places Chapter 29, pages 265-267 - Signposts). The author F. LaGard Smith talks about signposts along many walking paths in the Cotswolds of England. Many of the paths are hidden by time and nature.

"When I first started walking in the Cotswolds, I often found myself lost, confused and finding myself back where I had been for hours... Recognizing the difficulty of finding one's way along unfamiliar footpaths makes me appreciate all the more the life of Jesus. Having a personal guide, rather than simply printed guidelines, makes all the difference. Having that personal touch makes all the difference. In Jesus we have a reliable guide in whose footsteps we can confidently follow. When Jesus called the chosen Twelve saying 'Follow Me,' He was also calling us saying, 'Follow Me for I am the Way'."

If you were to say to me that following Jesus is not always easy, I would have to agree with you. Invariably he insists on taking me along the highest path - the one that stretches every fiber of my being. Nevertheless, wherever he leads, I know it's the right path.

This leads into what Pastor Mark Bates talked about this past Sunday, the Second Advent Sunday titled *Joseph's Story* based on Matthew 1:18-25. Joseph was a just man and was unwilling to put Mary to shame so he was going to divorce her quietly. But an angel of the Lord appeared to him in a dream and told him not to fear and take Mary as his wife (what an unfamiliar path that was for Joseph). Jesus came into this world to save his people from their sins.

Joseph was also willing to name the baby Mary was carrying. The angel told him to name the child "Immanuel" (which means God is with us).

As Pastor Mark Bates said, "Jesus entered this messy world to lift us up knowing he won't make it out alive. That's how much he loves us!"

Thinking about Joseph, God certainly took him as well as Mary on paths they didn't know. Mary being about fifteen years of age, pregnant and a virgin. Joseph not much older between eighteen and twenty, finding out his bride-to-be was pregnant, knowing the baby wasn't his, but willing to wed her. Both of them had an encounter with the Living God and both were willing to follow Him on "paths they didn't know".

Jesus entered my own messy life some 34 years ago. I was going through a divorce and facing the future with a two year old son to raise. Jesus said, "Follow me for you are My child." That was an unfamiliar path.

Looking back on that path, I am fine and my son Jason is more than fine! His wife, Tara is great and their daughter (my granddaughter) Emerson is perfect.

There have been smaller unfamiliar paths over the years and some rather large ones. This Cancer journey an unfamiliar path to be sure. He is showing me many treasures that are like picking a bouquet of wild flowers, each one of thankfulness that I am doing my best to give back to Him as a praise. He is healing me on many levels, showing me His great love for me and how to be a better witness for Him to name a few.

Don't be afraid to go on unfamiliar paths. Jesus calls you to: Cancer, the death of a loved one, broken family relationships, surgeries, children who decide for "a season" to go their own way, leaving family and friends for a job in another state, to name a few.

"Jesus will be your guide and the bouquet you will be willing to pick along the way will be a sweet smelling aroma to Him. Remember He said, 'I will never leave you nor forsake you.'" (Hebrews 13:5b) He also said, *"He would never leave you."* (John 14:18; Psalm 27:9,10; Isaiah 42:16; Deuteronomy 31:6,8; Joshua 1:5)

Next Chemo is this Friday, the 9th at 9:30. Thank you for your prayers as we travel this unfamiliar path together. Only one more after this one! The 30th. It has gone quick, hasn't it???!! Maybe because I have tried really hard to have a smile on my face, a bounce in my step, do what all my doctors tell me to do and keeping my eyes on Jesus.

There have been times that I do get down. I ask Jesus to please show me regardless how small it is how much He loves me or the beauty of His creation... and He always does... the early morning walks with Annie, my dog when the sky is just starting to see the sun or feeding the horses and one will nudge me with its head, or Jason will call, or I will see one of the many Emerson pictures I have around the house and I say, "Ahhhhhhh, life IS good isn't it, Jesus?" And He always answers, "Yes, My child, it is."

Isaiah 52:12

T.

December 7th
Email inbox: from Scott Vaughn

What an encouraging read! What a blessing that you can encourage all of us in the midst of your trials. Thank you. Jesus. I love the altar that you have built to remember God's mighty work in your life all along the way. HE is faithful to complete the work He has begun. Once again you so readily reflect what I prayed for you in *Jesus Calling* today.

"Learn to look steadily at Me in all your moments and in all your circumstance. Though the world is unstable and in flux, you can experience continuity through your uninterrupted awareness of My presence."

Email inbox: from Ed Altman

Your amazing strength and grace through all these very trying circumstances truly astounds me. Now I am fully aware of where you draw your strength from; but, it still astounds me. A lesser person such as me would have crumbled long ago. Terry, YOU are one of the most amazing persons I have ever met. When your ordeal is successfully over, I must come down to take you to lunch or dinner to celebrate. You are in my daily prayers; but FRIDAY I will have an extra session, Bible in hand, for Miss Terry!!!

Email outbox: December 9th

Good Afternoon:

Just got home from #3.Took longer than usual because it was #3 and the drip of chemo was slower as I had some in me from having gone for three weeks. It's like a triple hit to the system. I am feeling great! Isn't God amazing???!!! One more on the 30th and that's it for the chemo party. Yahoo Baby!!!

Email inbox: from Scott Vaughn

Thanks for sharing, Terry. It's a blessing to be watching as God meets you so consistently, even in unexpected ways, in the midst of your deepest concerns, and gently stretches you into His good and perfect will. And He is speaking so powerfully into all our lives through your journey.

From my Prayer Journal
December 12th

"I am taking care of you. Feel the warmth and security of being enveloped in my loving presence. Every detail of your life is under My control. If you could only see on your behalf, you would never again doubt that I am wonderfully caring for you. This is why you must live by faith, not by sight, trusting in My mysterious majestic presence." (From Jesus Calling, page 363. Based on Romans 8:28; 1 Peter 5:7; 2 Corinthians 5:7)

Thank you Jesus, for your loving humble ways as King of Kings - The Great I Am - who is a tear-wiping King and a promise-keeping king (from teachings at Village 7 Presbyterian by Bryan Counts). You win every battle. I am thankful I am your child as the crossroads get closer. I want to continue to walk holding your hand, a sheep walking next to her Shepherd trusting and loving You with each step.

From my Prayer Journal
December 14th

From DAILY BREAD:

"A man has nothing better under the sun than to eat, drink, and be merry, for this will remain with him in his labor all the days of his life." (Ecclesiastes 2:11)

A popular slogan says, 'Life is not measured by the number of breaths we take, but by the moments that take our breath away.' If we measure life by breathtaking moments, we miss the wonder of ordinary moments. Eating, sleeping, and breathing seem "ordinary" in that we do them every day without much thought. But they are not ordinary at all. Every bite and every breath are miracles.

King Solomon may have had more breath-taking moments than anyone. He said, "I did not withhold my heart from any pleasure." (Ecclesiastes 2:10). But he expressed cynicism about it by saying, "All of it is meaningless." (Ecclesiastes 2:17)

"Solomon's life reminds us that it's important to find joy in 'ordinary' things, for they are indeed wonderful. Bigger is not always better. More is not always an improvement (sometimes it's just more). Busier doesn't make us more important."

As I read this I thought of other ordinary moments sitting at my kitchen table: a squirrel scurrying up a tree; a bird setting on the edge of a bird bath sipping water; emails, phone calls and texts from family and friends, just to check in to see how I am feeling.

The ordinary is good... No, it is great!

I am told I am doing well. I believe that. God is doing amazing things in my life and for others I am told who read these emails. I am not in some great battle (so many with Cancer and after the fact call it a battle or that they survived. I have yet to hear the word "healed". I think that is strange. I am learning how to sit quietly at the feet of the Great I Am allowing Him, maybe for the first time in my life, to have His way. I, as always, the one to say, "Yeah but God what about this?" or "Let me do it, OK?" or "Lord, I really know what to do, honest. Listen to my idea."

But now in the quietness of God regardless of the circumstance or problems, I am learning to offer up a prayer before I make a decision. Shocking, I know. I sense a crossroad is coming. I pray I will choose not to waste this time, this Cancer journey, that I don't think of it as a broken leg or as many say, "I survived." and go on with their lives. I want to walk as a sheep close to her Shepherd, never taking anything for granted and enjoying all the ordinary moments life has to offer. At rest and at peace.

When I think of rest and peace in circumstances I think of the question someone asked me: Is it a mother bird feeding her baby chicks in a nest on a small tree limb next to a raging waterfall or is it a calm, still, placid lake with a fisherman in the boat fishing?

The answer is the bird and her young. I want to be that bird, doing the ordinary with trust regardless of life's circumstances. Again and always, thank you for your prayers. Praying for you.

Psalm 23

T.

December 14th
Email inbox: from Karen Hulbert

Remember that God takes the Ordinary and turns them into Extraordinary. He is the Extra and we are the ordinary. Remember He is Super and we are natural, so we become supernatural with Him!

Email inbox: from Mary Griffioen

Terry, this sets me back on my heels. You have struck a tender spot. The fact that you are allowing the Lord to bring you willingly to this quiet place and speak to you is something wonderful. I want this kind of relationship with the Father. I had that once but have let work and busyness get in the way. I miss that place. Thank you for allowing the Father to use you in this way. I hope that many hearts are changed because of what you are experiencing.

From my Prayer Journal
December 16th

"He brought me forth also into a broad place; He rescued me, because He delights in me." (Psalm 18:19) and in Song of Solomon 7:6: *"How beautiful and delightful you are."*

In 7:10: *"I am my beloved's and he desires it for me."*

In Psalm 41:11: *"By this I know that Thou aren't pleased with me, because my enemy does not shout in triumph over me."*

I am thankful to you O Lord, who delights in me. Your love over me is a banner, You want me in a broad place. You heal me for I am Yours, You swing me in Your arms, laughing. Thank you. I am Your sheep to always see the ordinary things as great, to continue in trust and quietness, knowing you always have my best in mind. Thank you for healing. Thank you for only one more chemo on the 30th.

Email outbox: December 22nd

Good Morning:

"I will never leave you nor forsake you." Hebrews 13:5

"All is well, all is well.
Angels and men rejoice!
For tonight darkness fell
Into the dawn of love's light.
Sing alle, sing alle!
All is well, all is well.
Let there be peace on earth.
Christ is come.
Go and tell that he is in the manger.
Sing alle, sing alleluia!
All is well, all is well.
Lift up your voice and sing, sing.
Born is now Emmanuel.

Born is our Lord and Savior.
Sing alleluia! Sing alleluia!
All is well. All is well."

(Words by Wayne Kirkpatrick, Music by Michael W. Smith. Warner/Chappell Music, Inc. Universal Music Publishing)

From Daily Bread: *"To hear the words of that song at Christmas time is comforting to many. But some people are unable to absorb the message because their lives are in turmoil. Their hearts loudly cry out. "All is not well-for me!" But for those of us who celebrate the birth of our Savior - despite the dark night of the soul we may experienced - all is well because of Christ. God is beside us and promises never to leave."* (Hebrews 13:5).

"He promises His grace is sufficient." (2 Corinthians 12:90)

"He promises to supply all our needs." (Philippians 4:19)

"He promises us the amazing gift of eternal life." (John 10:27-28).

Looking back to August when this Cancer journey began I can say, "All is well: God has fulfilled His promises and then some."

In fact it has been well since the beginning. God knew what I needed and just how much. He weighs the scales of trials very carefully and gives grace in abundance without measure; grace upon grace. Only one chemo left, next week the 30th! Thank you for your prayers and support!

Love you all...

Psalm 46:1-3

T.

Closing thought:

"Before me, even as behind, God is, and all is well." John Greenleaf Whittier

**From my Prayer Journal
December 30th**

Thank you Lord, that today is the last chemo. Thank you for carrying me and healing me.

Thank you for leading me. That is unique for me, that I can trust and love you more - drawing closer to you I am becoming the person I should be, my true self, one of a kind, on a solitary path while staying in close contact with others (to finish my books?) to freely love others.

I marvel at the beauty of my life intertwined with you, rejoicing always in the adventure I am having with you. Looking back over the year, it has been an adventure and next year will be exciting. You know the road and are holding my hand. That is all I need to know.

Email outbox: December 30th

Good Afternoon:

"Let us go with you, because we have heard that God is with you." (Zechariah 8:23)

"A heart that is hungry to know God resides in each person. When others see God, in us they want to come along. What they hear and see as they accompany us determines if they want to join us for the rest of the journey home" (From the Hungry Heart by Jan Carlberg)

Today was the last chemo. I felt relief and release as I drove home. I cried. I have grown in trust and love for The LORD! I have no side effects and laugh and enjoy life more than I have in a long time and yet the tears flowed as I drove home.

As I told you all in the beginning, I have prayed that you and those I see in the chemo lab and the doctor's office would see Jesus in me and want to know more about Him. I still pray that as I have "time off" before the surgery at the end of January. Not sure when, will let you know the details when I know them. I would assume my surgeon will call in the next week or two and let me know.

Please continue to pray. I am out of the forest of chemo and about ready to walk into another forest - surgery. I will continue to email to keep you updated. I am going to save these emails as a foundation for a book to encourage others.

I am going to see *War Horse* tonight - by myself - since I have been teary-eyed over the last chemo and those who know me know I cry in movies... a lot! There are only three people who will go to the movies with me: my son, who lives in Windsor, Colorado and two good friends who both said, "Not *that* movie and are *you* really going to see *that* one?" So who will know if I am crying over the end of chemo or the movie? I have cried at the trailers of *War Horse* so I am sure this is a full tissue box movie night.

Isaiah 49:16

T.

December 31st
Email inbox: from Ed Altman

Read HABAKKUK 3:18.19: *"Yet I will rejoice in the LORD, I will joy in the GOD of my salvation. The Lord God is my strength; He will make my feet like deer's feet, and HE will make me walk on my high hills."*

Since your CHEMO is finished, please rejoice and give thanks to THE LORD who has provided you with tremendous strength and a positive happy frame of mind. I share your relief that this trying stage is done.

Email inbox: from Sherri Schmallen

You continue to inspire and impress me. You are truly amazing. Thank you for expressing your Journey so openly and full of love and trust. Happy New Year.

CHAPTER 7 - JANUARY

Email outbox: January 1st

Good Morning:

"Thus far has the LORD helped us." 1 Samuel 7:12

The words "thus far" seems like a hand pointing in the direction of the past - through poverty, through wealth, through sickness, through health, at home, abroad, on the land, on the sea, in honor, in dishonor, in perplexity, in joy, at home, in temptation.

"Thus far the LORD helped us!"

But the word also points forward. For when one arrives at a certain mark and writes "Thus far," one is not yet at the end. More joys, more temptations, more triumphs, more prayers, more answers, more toils, more strength, more fights, more victories, and then comes sickness, old age, disease, death.

Is it over now? No! There is still more, awaking in Jesus' likeness, thrones, harps, songs, psalms, white clothing, the face of Jesus, the society of saints, the glory of God, the fullness of eternity, and the infinity of bliss.

"O be of good courage, believer, and with grateful confidence raise your 'Ebenezer'. Thus far as the LORD helped us, for He who hath helped thee hitherto will help

thee all thy journey through." (From Morning and Evening by Charles H. Spurgeon, page 728)

I am sure each of you can look back and say, "thus far has the LORD helped us". Isn't that exciting? And He will do that again this year!

Looking forward to the end of the Cancer journey in March and thanking you in advance for standing in prayer for me.

Closing thought:

"I waited patiently for the LORD; and He inclined to me, and heard my cry. He also brought me up out of a horrible pit. Out of the miry clay, and set my feet upon a rock, and established my steps. He has put a new song in my mouth- praise to our God; many will see it and fear, and will trust in the LORD." (Psalm 40:1-3)

Happy New Year! Love you all, praying for you

T.

Email outbox: January 5th

Good Afternoon:

"Jesus himself drew near, and went with them." Luke 24:15

"Jesus never sends a man ahead alone. He blazes a clear way through every thicket and woods, and then softly calls, 'Follow me. Let us go on together, you and I.' He has been everywhere that we are called to go. His feet have trodden down smooth a path through every experience that comes to us. He knows each road, and knows it well: the valley road of disappointment with its dark shadows; the steep path of temptation down through the rocky ravines and slippery gullies; the narrow path of pain with the brambly thorn-bushes as close to each side, with their slash and sting; the dizzy road along the heights of victory; the old beaten road of commonplace daily routine. Every path He has trodden and glorified and will walk anew with each of us. The only safe way to travel is with Him alongside and in control." (From Springs in the Valley, page 11)

The past four days have been hard. I have had asthma really bad and a chest cold, coughing up the nasty mucus. There aren't enough tissues. I am carrying a roll of toilet paper with me... Easier. I am somewhat better today... not great.

I read the above sometime this week and thought how Jesus knew what road I needed to take at this season in my life. He went before me before the foundation of the world and chose the roads I needed to travel and when.

I am grateful I didn't know the road until my foot was on it. Can you image knowing your life before it happens? How awful would that be? Divorce, death of family members, relationships broken that no matter what you do nothing works to fix them, car accidents, Cancer to name a few. I am so grateful that in His perfect time the road shows itself and he smiles and says, "Let us go. I will lead. You follow." And I will hold His hand as he is holding mine and off we go.

It seems so quiet today. I don't have Rush or Hannity on the radio or music or a great black and white movie. Trying to get well. I started reading the emails I have sent since the beginning. My, how I have grown in my walk with Jesus! I think for now I am going to type them out, add my Truth Cards and Prayer Journal notes and keep all in order of when they happened.

Thank you for your prayers. They are working!

Romans 8:28

T.

Closing thought:

"All tomorrows of our lives have to pass before HIM before they can get to us." (From Springs in the Valley, page 13)

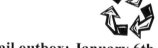

Email outbox: January 6th

Good Morning:

I just talked to my breast surgeon's office and I see her on January 24th. At that time we will talk about the date of surgery and what to expect. Will keep you informed as I know more at that time.

I am so grateful for all your prayers and walking with me on this journey. There were no side effects at all with chemo - a little tired and a headache here and there but that was it!

Soon phase two will be done, then surgery, and on to the last phase of radiology (if needed) and then it is all done! Then a party at my house! My hair is coming back rather fast I think, the sides and back have color and the top is a hint of a soft fuzz of color.

And now the drum roll... the color is black!!! Yes, black! Who would have thought?!

"My heart overflows with a good theme; I address my verses to the King; My tongue is the pen of a ready writer."
Psalm 45:1

T.

January 12th
Email inbox: from Cathy Sparks

Smiles, hope and joy in reading this email! Thanks for being so open with us all. Helps us pray!

From my Prayer Journal
January 13th

I will look at each day as an adventure with you, Jesus. I will look forward to what you have prepared for me. Life is precious and a repeatable gift. Walking close to you is never dull or predictable. Look at the past six months. Cancer and enjoying life. Only with you could I smile on this road. My hair is coming back and the color is black. What a surprise! I want to be willing to follow you no matter how steep or treacherous the path. The safest place is by your side. (Based on Psalm 118:24; 1 Peter 2:12 from Jesus Calling)

Soon... Surgery in a few weeks. I see Dr. Paulishak on the 24th. I ask all will go well with no complications.

January 14th
Email inbox: from Mary Griffioen

Love the scripture quote. Black hair. That will be different. What a great idea, writing a book of your journey. I have kept almost all of your responses to us. As I said before, they have been helpful for me in my everyday life, nothing compared to what you are walking through. Your emails have encouraged me to keep you lifted before the Father's throne. I look forward to your emails.

From my Prayer Journal
January 18th

"Whom shall I send? And who will go for us? And I said, 'Here am I. Send me'." (Isaiah 6:8)

Lord, I want to be giving You a cup of water, to be an encouragement to others – write a book based on the emails? Please guide me as I move forward with this idea.

"He putteth forth his own sheep." (John 10:4)

Thank you that you are in all my tomorrows before the sun rises each day for me. Surgery is coming up. Please let it be uneventful. I was not to stay where I was in August pre-Cancer. Your loving hand pushed me out on a road trip with you. I will be forever changed, hopefully for the better. I want to stay close to you - hearing your voice, clear and true. (Based on Streams in the Desert, page 23)

Thank you that I am fully understood and known by you. You know me better than I know myself. I enjoy sharing my fears and struggles with you and you are transforming my weakness into strengths. Thank you that you cover me with your grace and mercy and forgive me of my sins.

"I am leading you along the high road, but there are descents as well as ascents. Learn to trust Me when things go 'wrong'. Disruptions to your routine highlight your dependence on Me. Trust does not falter when the path

becomes rocky and steep. Breathe deep draughts of My Presence, and hold tightly to My hand. Together we can move it!" (Jesus Calling, based on John 2:19; 2 Corinthians 4:17; Habakkuk 3:19, page 19)

Thank you for leading me on the high road - close, holding your hand. I want to be pleasing to/with you, that you will say, "Well done, well done my child." I pray the surgery will be successful and uneventful and it will prove the Cancer is gone. Thank you healing me. Please bless and encourage those who are praying for me.

From my Prayer Journal
January 20th

"Approach this day with awareness of who is Boss. It is who orchestrates the events of your life... When things go smoothly according to your plans you may be unaware of My sovereign Presence. On days when your plans are thwarted, be on the lookout for Me! It is essential at such times to stay in communication with me, accepting My way as better than yours. Don't try to figure out what is happening. Simply trust Me and thank Me in advance for the good that will come out of it all. I know the plans I have for you and they are good." (Jesus Calling, based on Isaiah 55:9-11 and Jeremiah 29:11, page 21)

Looking back over these past few months of the Cancer journey and ahead to surgery and then radiation the above is true. I would never have penciled chemotherapy as something on my "to do list," Lord, but you did and I must admit we have had some pretty good talks, haven't we?

I learned that I can't figure anything out; Cancer, family, work, anything. But You can and do. I ask that the surgery will go well and be uneventful, the drains will be for the shortest time possible, and most importantly the surgery and the biopsy will show the Cancer is gone – totally.

Thank you, Jesus. There will be (there already is) good coming out of this Cancer journey we are on. A closer walk with You; others are seeing you in me – a book to encourage others.

Thank you for your prayers... I feel undeserving but needing Job 2:10

T.

Email outbox: January 24th

Good Evening:

I saw Dr. Paulishak today. Surgery will be on February 8th. I need to there at 6 AM. I will be there overnight. I am not telling you where as I don't want cards, flowers, and most importantly I don't want visitors. I think I have always believed if you are in the hospital you are to get well and not entertain someone with a smile on your face. I don't mean to be rude. I would like and need your prayers.

During my visit the Doctor gave me two choices; The first was to go in and remove what is left. (There is a small "something" - could be Cancer or not). That would be out-patient.

BUT, if she didn't get it all then another surgery will be needed soon. It (the Cancer?) is close to the nipple and that makes it hard. And there would be a 30% change of return.

My second choice is a full mastectomy to make sure she got it. There is a 7% change of return.

For me the negatives are spending the night in the hospital and the physical drain that could last a week or so. I am so bloody independent (she told me that).

I told her to schedule the surgery for a full mastectomy as of now. She is going to call in a few days to confirm. She also said that my radiologist said when she talked to me in August before it all started that she was borderline if I needed radiology or not. Dr. Paulishak will talk to her and let me know. Having a full mastectomy and chemo and what is left is at .5 could mean I won't need it.

It has been a hard few days for me for several issues. My asthma is alive and well. My voice was gone but it is slowly coming back. I have had a cold (if that is the right word) in my lungs, getting better...

The surgery is on the 8th. Hopefully and prayerfully, I won't have to change it. My lungs must be clear.

And other issues of doubting God... How could I, after all He has done for me. And yet I struggle. I feel like a backslider for my doubts and anger toward the issues at hand. Maybe I am too reformed in my faith... I know God allows trials, He doesn't tempt but He does allow... and I know if we confess, that He is faithful to forgive... I have confessed, but still feel dull and empty.

To be honest, the two things I wrote Sunday night thinking and knowing they are a great encouragement before the doubts and anger... Maybe I should read them out loud to myself. I would like to share a couple of things with you.

The words to "He Never Failed Me Yet." by Robert Bay. We sang this song Sunday in church. It is a hand clapping, body-swaying song. (Was I really at Village 7)???

The following words are so good!

"I will sing of God's Mercy. Every day, every hour he gives me power. I will sing and give thanks to thee for all the dangers, toils and snares that he has brought me out. He is my God and I'll serve him, no matter what the test. Trust and never doubt. Jesus will surely bring you out. He never failed me yet. I know God is able to deliver in time of storm. I know that he'll keep you from all earthy harm. One day when my weary soul is at rest, I'm going home to be forever bless'd. Trust and never doubt. Jesus will surely bring you out. He never failed me yet. Didn't my God deliver Moses from King Pharaoh? And didn't he cool the fiery furnace for Shadrach, Meshach, and Abednego? When I think of what my God can do, he delivered Daniel, I know he will deliver you. Trust and never doubt, Jesus will surely bring you out, he never failed me yet."

January 29th
Inbound email: from Joy Lundy

Hang in there, Terry. You've been through a lot and have been so strong. This has been a long process, that is for sure. We have been studying I and II Thessalonians and the prayers that Paul gave in both of them is wonderful. I especially like the prayer in II Thessalonians 2:15-17.

"Stand firm and hold to the teachings we passed on to you, whether by word of mouth or letter. May our Lord Jesus Christ himself and God our Father, who loved us and by his grace gave us eternal encouragement and good hope, encourage your hearts and strength you in every good deed and word."

Inbound email: from Carl Nelson

What a journey you are in the midst of Terry. It is good to hear of your struggles and fears but what joy to hear of your faith and trust. May you ever rest in the shelter of His wings.

Email outbox: January 31st

Some thoughts from my prayer journal I would like to share with you...

As I look toward surgery on February 8th I ask my lungs be totally clear. I am thankful you are Lord, the Great I Am, The Lord Who Heals, Jehovah-Rapha. I am trusting you as your thoughts are precious towards me and vast in numbers (Psalm 139:17)

Thank you that you have my day planned out long before I wake up. I need to stay focused on you and not wonder or worry about what is on the road ahead. When I do start to feel afraid I will remember you are my shield - a shield that is always alert and active, not inanimate armor. Thank you for protecting me from known and unknown dangers - you will watch over me wherever I go.

"So you will walk in the way of good men, and keep to the paths of the righteous." Proverbs 2:20.

Closing thought:

"Resolved, to live with all my might while I do live. Resolved, never to lose one moment of time, to improve it in the most profitable way I possibly can. Resolved never to do anything which I should despise or think meanly of in another. Resolved, never to do anything which I should be afraid to do if it were the last hour of my life." Jonathan Edwards

Thank you for your prayers on the 8th. Soon it will be over! Oh happy day!

2 Corinthians 2:15

T.

CHAPTER 8 – FEBRUARY

Email outbox: February 2nd

Good Evening:

I can't remember if I told you that I have had a very bad chest cold. Voice gone, asthma, and lungs filled with junk. I saw my primary care doctor today and my lungs are totally clear. He listened to all three areas of my right lung. I think he listened for ten to fifteen minutes and all is good.

My voice is still not there but it is coming back and almost normal. That being said, surgery is on February the 8th. I need to be there at 6 AM and surgery is at 8. I will be there for one night and home the next day. I will email you when I get home. Thank you in advance for your prayers. I won't know about radiation until after surgery and they will look at all the breast tissue at that time. Will let you know when I know.

February 4th
Inbound email: from Ed Altman

I thought the following might give you strength, courage, and good health for the week of February 6, 2012.

"Rejoice in the LORD always. I will say it again: Rejoice! Let your gentleness be evident to all, The Lord is near. Do

not be anxious about anything but in everything, by prayer and petition with thanksgiving, present your requests to GOD. And the peace of God, which transcends all understanding, will guard your hearts and minds in CHRIST JESUS." Philippians 4:4-7

"Gracious is the LORD, and righteous: yes, our GOD is merciful. The LORD preserves the simple; I was brought low, and HE saved me." Psalm 34: 1-4. *"I will extol the LORD at all times; his praise will always be on my lips. My soul will boast in the LORD; let the afflicted hear and rejoice. Glorify the LORD with me; let us exalt his name together. I sought the LORD, and he answered me; HE delivered me from all my fear."* Psalm 116: 5, 6.

Inbound email: from Erin Lockett

May the gates of heaven be flooded with prayers that day my friend! Looking forward to hearing about how wonderfully you are doing afterward!

Email outbox: February 7th

Good Afternoon:

Tomorrow is the day. Surgery at 8am. Please pray for the following:

No complications

No after-effects

The drain will be easy to manage

The drain will only be for a week.

I see Dr. Paulishak on the 14th (Happy Valentines' Day)!

This past Sunday we sang *"Grace Flows Down"*. I loved the words so I want to share.

"Amazing Grace, how sweet the sound
Amazing love, now flowing down
From hands and feet that were nailed to the tree
As grace flows down and covers me
It covers me, It covers me
It covers me and covers me."

Thank you again and again for walking with me on this road with your prayers. YOU are amazing to have lasted this long with me! I will be spending tomorrow night there (Wednesday). Home on Thursday. I will email you all then.

Psalm 1:1-3

T.

Closing thought:

"Aim at heaven, and you will get earth thrown in. Aim at earth, and you will get neither." C.S. Lewis

February 7th
Inbound email: from Bonnie McGowan

I'm praying for you. Know this is an unnerving time. Know too, that God is holding you tight even though you're shaking in your boots. I'm praying perfect peace that only He can give in the midst of this horrific storm. Soon there will be peace and calming.

Psalm 4:8 *"I will lie down and sleep in peace, for alone, oh Lord, make me dwell in safety."*

Inbound email: from Sari Brian

Lord Jesus, Thank You for Terry and her great faith. It has changed my life! I pray in agreement with her that tomorrow the surgery will be so easy for her that she will be shocked. Just like with the chemo sessions. I pray for no complications, no after effects, that the drain will be so easy to manage she won't believe it and will come out exactly as planned in one week. Father, when she sees the doctor on February 14th I pray that she will be feeling so well that Dr. Paulishak will be amazed and praise God with her in that appointment. And Lord I pray that there will be no pain at all, that she will be peaceful and comfortable and able to rest tonight, too, as well as after the surgery. Keep her mind on You, my Lord, and walk her through this surgery hand-in-hand, I pray. Cause the doctor to have the best sleep and rest of her life tonight and be sharp and alert all through the surgery. Cause her mind to be focused, intent, and full of Your wisdom as she proceeds with this surgery. And Father, when it is over I pray that there will be absolutely nothing left of the Cancer - not even one cell's worth, that this will be the end of the end of the story, and that the Cancer will never-ever return! In Jesus' name.

Amen

Inbound email: from Carolyn Moritz

My Dear sister friend, T - Your email arrived! I am well aware of tomorrow. The date has been locked in my heart - Tonight on this Tuesday vigil, Chris and I will offer our Evening Prayer for you! Your specific prayer requests are much appreciated. As we walk the path together - on the WAY!! God Bless you and the doctors and nurses and all the care-givers tomorrow. You are our miracle!

Inbound email: from Brad and Lynn Bowles

Love you, really! Been reading emails and praying throughout all of this with you. You are awesome. Wait! That should be reserved for God. You are what Sheila Walsh's song, *"The Warrior is a Child"* is all about because you run to Him, your strength is constantly being renewed. So know that I will be one of many lifting you up in prayer tomorrow. Thank you for being modern day David... i.e. your musing put to paper? Key strokes? However you do it.

Email outbox: February 9th

Good Morning:

Just got home a little while ago. No pain, no pain pills. The only pain killers were in the IV during surgery. After surgery my IV had two drips: one was a saline solution, the other was an antibiotic.

God is so good, isn't he?

I had to be there yesterday at 6:15 in the morning. Not sure why as I had done pre-registration. At 7:30 a nurse came and got me and the surgery started right at 8. I woke up in recovery at 10. Jason had court in Castle Rock earlier and came walking in while I was in recovery. It was fun to see him.

A friend of mine had a mastectomy and was in Memorial North. I was at Printer's Parkway (who knew they had beds). There is a major difference between the two. Memorial North is like a small five star hotel. It has maybe sixty rooms and the food service is called room service (anytime you would like something just pick up the phone).

Memorial North offers a full menu all the time from fresh salmon to meatloaf with mashed potatoes and milkshakes or chocolate cake.

I on the other hand, was at Printer's Parkway. It's more like camping with a picnic lunch or dinner (sandwich, chips, fruit and a cookie) served up in a box! But it was so much fun I wouldn't have wanted to be anywhere else.

Yesterday late afternoon, I asked the nurse if I could have some coffee. She had a deer in the headlights look and said she didn't know how to make coffee. I told her I would be glad to show her how to make it. She just laughed and said, "I think I can figure it out. The coffee is pre-measured and all I have to do is press a button." She did a great job!

I was the only one there last night! There were two nurses (had to have two at night) I guess because during the day there is a whole building of people and if something went wrong with a patient, two nurses would be good. We laughed a lot. One took me on a walk around the recovery and pre-surgery areas, a big circle that we did several times... It was good to go on a "real walk".

After the nurses checked the IV, took vitals and oxygen levels, and wrapped my legs to make sure no blood clots happened, sleep was a good idea. Before I dozed off, I told the nurses they needed board games. They thought that was a good idea. One has three little girls around Emerson's age so we talked about little girls and Fancy Nancy books.

When the morning nurse came in, she asked what the patient was like (to know what she was walking into). They said they had never had a patient like me... no pain or complaining. She laughed a lot and offered to make coffee before they came on duty. I even stripped the bed this morning and put the sheets and towels in the "used laundry" container.

Bryan Counts, a pastor from my church stopped by. He read Psalm 139 and we prayed. We laughed a lot and I gave my testimony on becoming a Christian. I told him I had planned on taking the Inquirer's Class the previous fall (to be a member of the Church) and a Bible study (time to get "back in the game") but then this Cancer came along. He said, "God had a different road for you, now didn't He?" I said, "Yes, He did."

Friday (tomorrow) I get to have a shower and take the bandages off and wear a sports bra until the stitches come out... smiling! I see the doctor on the 14th as follow-up from the surgery and hopefully the drain will come out at that time.

"For in the day of trouble He will conceal me in His tabernacle; in the secret place of His tent He will hide me; He will lift me upon a rock." (Psalm 27:5)

A note I have in my Bible from some teaching says, *"Although storms come into our lives never for a second will they alter God's plan for our lives."*

Thank you for praying for me... you are the best!!!!

Song of Solomon 2:4

T.

February 9th
Inbound email: from Deena Stuart

My heart sings! Praise to the Lord, the Almighty, the King of Creation. Oh my soul, praise Him for He is thy help and Salvation! All ye who hear, now to His temple draw near. Join me in glad adoration. We continue in our prayers for no more Cancer.

Email outbox: February 14th

Happy Valentine's Day! I see Dr. Paulishak at 2:30. Please pray ALL Cancer is gone and I don't need radiation. I also would like the drain out but to be honest I have my doubts. She told me that there is a fine line when it comes to the drain. If I exercise too much or not at all, the drain will stay in two extra weeks. You know how I am. I like to exercise.

I started back to caring for the horses on Friday and walking Annie three times a day plus other normal arm movements.

The amount of fluid in the drain has to be below 25 on the last day. It was 22 on Sunday, but yesterday it was 36. Today I have morning and afternoon numbers to give the doctor (and empty the bag three times a day). If I have another week that's okay. All the bandages are off and taking a shower is wonderful!

Have a great day with Jesus.

T.

Email 2 - outbox: February 14th

Good Afternoon:

The Cancer is gone... Yep... Gone !!

"The small something" was a .9 Cancer but with the mastectomy it is gone and it wasn't close to the margins.

I see the radiologist on Feb. 22nd to see if I need radiation. Dr. Paulishak doesn't think I will as the Cancer is gone and it wasn't close to the margins. But Dr Ridings will make the call.

Please pray no radiation is needed. I still have the drain until this Thursday or Friday. The number needs to be down below 30 (not 25). That helps. I am to call Thursday (assuming it is below 30) and make an appointment for her to take the drain out. I am so excited! I cried on the way home (so what else is new Terry)?

"Now to Him who is able to do exceeding abundantly beyond all that we ask or think, according to the power that works within us." (Ephesians 3:20)

"For as the heavens are higher than the earth, so are My ways higher than your ways, and My thoughts than your thoughts." and Jeremiah 29:11: *"For I know the plans that I have for you, declares the LORD, plans for welfare and not for calamity to give you a future and a hope."* Isaiah 55:9

Thank you for standing in the gap, praying for me!

Psalm 5:3

T.

February 14th
Inbound email: from Carolyn Mortiz

Happy St. Valentine's Day! Gift from God. Cancer Free. Music to your ears, our ears. Your loyal followers have prayed and your strength led us to this moment closer to Jesus! You are a strong woman in the LORD! Now go to bed and sleep in the peace of Christ. So will we! God bless your beautiful heart. Thank you for writing. You are foremost in my heart and I am so excited... Your beautiful spiritual insights and scripture. You are awesome in the LORD!!!!!! Let's cry tears together. My friend and dear friend, thank you for your email. God love ya.

Inbound email: from Ruth Mott

What a wonderful Valentine's Day gift your Beloved Jesus gave you! NO CANCER! I am praying with you that there be no radiation.

Email outbox: February 17th

Good Morning:

I just talked to Dr. Paulishak's office. I see her TODAY at 10:45 to have the drain out! It will take five minutes. Thank you for your prayers. Hopefully the last prayer request: NO radiation. I will know that on February 22nd.

Habakkuk 3:19

T.

February 17th
Inbound email: from Carolyn Mortiz

Pheeewwwww! My huge sigh of relief! You have amazing faith and an intercessory prayer team! Yes, yes, yes!!!

Drain out today! Hurray! You were called by God and you fought the good fight. God has rewarded your faithfulness and Trust in Him over this trial. You have raised us all up and carried us in your trial. We all share the reward! You are a wonderful friend and God put us together for this moment in time! Think of all those years ago to NOW! Thank you, God. Thank you, Jesus for my friend T!

1 Corinthians 6:17

Email outbox: February 18th

Good Afternoon:

The drain is out. I sat on the examining table. Dr. P. said, "Breathe and hold." I did and she pulled the tube out! And yes, it hurt!

I wore my special vest (for women with drains from breast surgery - ordered it from a Cancer catalog) for hopefully the last time. I couldn't tuck my turtle-necks or sweaters in my jeans. I even wore a bra to the doctor's office knowing I wasn't going to wear that vest again (going to donate it to her office for someone else to wear). A dear friend of mine remade my bras. She used old ones that didn't fit even before the Cancer journey for the right side. They look and feel normal except the right side on the inside is bigger. I showed the doctor's staff the one I was wearing and they were impressed.

I think I will take a quick spin on my horse Pop Pop. I haven't ridden since August.

154

You are the best!

T.

February 20th
Inbound email: from Ed Altman

Since I had today off, I concentrated on some prayers that I said for a favorable report from the radiologist for you. In reading my Bible I ran across a few items of scripture that I thought might help you as you approach what I will pray will be your final and last hurdle in the very long and so far successful ordeal.

1 Peter 5:6, 7: *"Humble yourselves, therefore, under God's mighty hand, that he may lift you up in due time. Cast all your anxiety on him because he cares for you."*

"May HE give you the desire of your heart and make all your plans succeed. We will shout for joy when you are victorious; and will lift up our banners in the name of our GOD. May the Lord grant all your requests." (Psalm 20.4, 5)

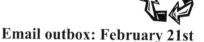

Email outbox: February 21st

Good Morning:

Please be praying for tomorrow, Wednesday the 22nd at 9:30, that I will not need radiation.

Thank you
Psalm 88:2

Closing thought:

"God's work only goes forward with prayer." (Dr. Don Sweeting, President of Reformed Theological Seminary in Orlando, Florida)

Email outbox: February 22nd

Good Afternoon:

Long, but worth the read, really!

This is from my favorite book (again); (Meeting God in Quiet Places by F. LaGard Smith, chapter 31, page 283)

Gravestone;

"Do those who walk through the graveyard notice the history beneath their feet? Do they stop to consider the faded aspirations and discarded status of those whose spent lives quietly rustle beneath their pounding footsteps?

As with most churchyards in England, the ground there is blanketed by ancient gravestones. Weatherworn and precariously tilting at odd angles, some of the old slates date back to the 1700's. A few of the gravestones tell interesting short stories about loved ones, as seen through the loving eyes of memory by those who survived. One of the most unusual and poignant inscriptions is found on a stone located on the west side of the church in the direction of the manor house;

Elizabeth Lee
1877-1960
Beloved nanny to three generations
Suffer little children to come unto me
And forbid them not, for such is the kingdom of heaven

I can only imagine a woman who, although she never married, was a mother to many. A woman of love and strength whose influence lives in the lives of those whose care was entrusted to her.

When I walk through these same gravestones, I can't help but think of Solomon's words;

'Generations come and generations go, but the earth remains forever - there is no remembrance of men of old, and even those who are yet to come will not be remembered by those who follow.'

No wonder Solomon was tempted to conclude that life - at least as we live it - is meaningless! As the world's wisest man, Solomon gives me little comfort in the thought that, no matter how special I might think I am, in generations to come no one will care. However what I do wonder about is whether the living will have made a difference. I suppose that family and friends would be kind enough to say that I had "touched their lives" while in their midst, but the same would be true of every individual who ever lived. Others are always affected for good or ill.

No, the question is whether there is any significant way in which I have touched the lives of others. Or as it is sometimes put, is the world better off for my having been here? What will be my legacy to future generations?

Perhaps the secret lies in thinking back on the significance of others who, by their simple acts of devotion or their desire for excellence, have helped us to dream big dreams and challenged us to reach beyond ourselves. When fears of eventful insignificance sweep over me, I always think of my high school English teacher, Sally R. Wilson.

It was Sally who taught me to write. Without her, who knows whether any of the words in my books ever would have surfaced to really make a difference in anyone's lives?

I think the same must be true of Sally's mother, a woman I never met, and whose name I never hear. Given that Sally's mother was "just a housewife," undoubtedly she too must have considered whether her obscure life would matter on the grand scale of things. But if it hadn't been for the sacrifices she made for Sally I might never have sat at Sally's feet.

Changed lives - that's what is ultimately important for each of us. That's what will truly last. The greatest good we may ever accomplish may be through someone else whose life we have influenced in seemingly insignificant ways.

We remember Peter as the one who preached so powerfully to the crowds gathered on Pentecost, but what about his brother, Andrew, who first told Peter about the Messiah?

And how could we forget the young evangelist, Timothy who was so instrumental in the spread of the gospel? But do we remember that his faith first lived in his grandmother Lois and in his mother Eunice?

We are reminded that there is a powerful influence for good that lies in the godly hand that rocks the cradle. There is no greater significance in all the world - whether for a father or a mother - than to bring up children "in the training and instruction of the Lord".

Changed lives are our greatest legacy. Changed lives are the gifts that truly keep on giving generation after generation. No matter how seemingly insignificant our own lives, we achieve significance through the lives that we touch for good. And never are our lives more significant than when the lives we touch are brought to know Christ. For at that point, lives are not simply changed but transformed! As you look back, who are those who have significantly touched your life at some point along the way?

If it's still possible, today might be a good day to let them know how much you appreciate it. And if you've ever wondered about your own significance, just look around you. Think of all the lives you are changing, or could change, even today.

Whether what I do is seen in the eyes of the world to be great or small, I only ask that when future generations pass unknowingly by my weathered gravestone, someone might be walking by on a different path because of something I have done. And not just a different path, but a higher one."
(F. LaGard Smith, Chapter 31, pgs. 284-288)

I know each of you have made a significant difference in my life. To say "thank you" seems too simple. This Cancer journey has been life-changing for me.

The simple easy things in life, what I once took for granted, are what are important to me now.

A smile.

The warmth of the sun on a snowy day.

Laughter across the room.

The smell of lavender and lilacs.

Watching the aspen leaves change color.

A phone call or text from Jason or Tara.

To hear Emerson's voice when I open their door.

As I think of working on a book, a quote from John Keith Falconer, that was in my church's bulletin this past Sunday, seems to apply:

"I have but one candle of life to burn, and I would rather burn it out in a land filled with darkness than in a land flooded with light."

I want to make a significant difference... this journey isn't going to waste.

Closing thought:

"As the blossom can't tell what becomes of its fragrance, we can't tell what becomes of our influence." (From Daily Bread)

2 Corinthians 2:15

T.

February 21st
Inbound email: from Deena Stuart

So good to hear your heart, dear Terry. Bob and I have often discussed the Lord's "severe mercy" in your life and that, like us, He loves you so much and has a great purpose for your life. I truly believe that the Lord MORE than matches our degree of suffering with His blessing and "joy (that) comes in the morning". We have seen you struggle to realize God the Father's love for you and it has been and will continue to be a joyful journey. We are coming into the Springs on Sunday night for three days and would love to see you, even for a hug, if you have the time. You are so precious to us and we count it an honor to have been in your inner circle of prayer.

Inbound email: from Jan Allums

Thank you, Terry. Definitely worth the read. Me think we live only to ourselves and affect only ourselves, but everything we do and are affects those around us. May we be worthy of our days that God has graciously given us.

Inbound email: from Shari Brain

Yea! Praise God you are healed!

My response:

When I read this, what you write. I started crying and the Lord quickened in my spirit that, yes, I am healed! Joy and praise to Him who is our God and Savior.

Inbound email: for Karen Hulbert

Praise God, He answered prayer! You are special and God loves you.

My response:

Thank you for standing with me!!!

Her response:

I love you and will always be there for you. May God use you as you share you HOPE with others.

Email outbox: February 22nd

Good Morning:

I saw Dr Riding this morning as you know and I do NOT need radiation!!!!! Smiling, crying. Praise the Lord!!!

Three memorable quotes: (Streams in the Desert, pages 59, 60)

"Though I have afflicted you, I will afflict you no longer." Nahum 1:12b

"There is a limit to affliction. God sends it and removes it. O, you sigh and say, 'When will the end be?' Let us quietly wait and patiently endure the will of the Lord till He cometh. Our Father takes away the rod when His design in using it is fully served. It is not hard for the Lord to turn night into day. He that sends the clouds can as easily clear the skies. Let us be of good cheer. It is better farther on. Let us sing Hallelujah by anticipation." Charles H. Spurgeon

"Be Patient, O sufferers! The result will more than compensate for all our trials, when we see how they wrought out the far more exceeding and eternal weight of glory. To have word of God's commendation: to be honored before the holy angels; to be gloried in Christ so as to be better able to flash His glory on Himself - ah! That will be more than repay for all." (From Tried By Fire)

"Nothing happens that has not been appointed with consummate care and foresight." (From Daily Devotional Commentary)

Thank you for unfailing prayers and support!

T.

Email outbox: February 23rd

Good Morning:
I am going to have an open house on the last Sunday in April from noon to three. I would like to send "real" invitations but email is easier and I don't have mailing addresses for most of you. I also want the church groups, prayer chains, staffs, that have prayed for me to attend... (Village 7 Presbyterian, The Church on the Ranch, Calvary Worship Center, Jason's and Tara's church and Leigh Ann's church.) They too are/will be invited along with spouses. I will send a reminder or two in March and April. Please RSVP.

I am also going to invite the chemo lab nurses and doctor's offices... a dandy group don't you think? I am going to have a chamber ensemble and light lunch stuff to eat and of course, champagne!

I had two goals in August, requests for the Lord: That Jesus would be seen in me and that I would be able to worship HIM in church every Sunday. The Lord not only answered those two requests but He gave me you as my prayer warriors and He healed me through your prayers!

I love you all more than you will know or words can say. You stood in the gap for eight months.

T.

February 24th

Inbound email: from Pastor Scott Vaughn

Good morning, Terry. We are praising God with you! He is so mighty to save and the sense that you have been in His loving grasp all along seems overwhelming this morning. Thank you Jesus!

Inbound email: from Zetta Henson

Party time INDEED!!! God is soooo Good!!! We love you, Terry and we know that you have been unselfishly praying for us and our families during a time in your life when you could easily be having a pity party for yourself. You should know that prayers are being answered in our lives, too. We know it is because of people like you that have stood with us, lifting us up, over and over again. We are grateful you are in our lives. But we do miss getting to look into your lives on a daily basis.

Inbound email: from Jackie Atkins

Oh, Terry! This is so powerful! I thank God that I have witnessed your journey and have been encouraged by the triumphant way He has led you through it. It is an amazing testament to what our God can do if we just "trust and obey"! The tears I am shedding now are tears of joy! God has blessed you my sister!

Inbound email: from Cathy Spark

You are an amazing daughter of the King! I have been so privileged to be a part of this journey with you. Looking forward to celebrating with you all that God has done on the last Sunday in April.

Inbound email: from Bonnie McGowan

I cried when I read this last page. What an ending to your beautiful book - what a blessing. I'm thankful I was able to learn about your journey these past months and am so thankful for the end of the Cancer and new beginning with life.

I am RSVPing "yes" to your open house the last Sunday in April. I will look forward to it and know I'll be blessed and cry a lot. Just seeing everyone with you, it will be heart-warming to see this praying family together.

Inbound email: from Mary Griffioen

What wonderful words you heard when you learned that you didn't have to have radiation. I can cry with you. Your journey has had such an impact on so many peoples' lives, mine included. I love the relationship you have with Jesus through all these months. Praise to the Father. You are an incredible woman. I've made a special folder of all your emails. I'll look through it when I need a reminder of God's faithfulness. May I have your permission to quote from them if it is appropriate? Continue to pray for you.

Inbound email: from Don See

I am Speechless! Your transparency, your faith, your support group! It is a joy and a privilege to know you. God bless you as He holds you in His hand.

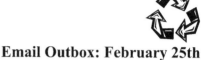

Email Outbox: February 25th

Yesterday I was told I will not need radiation. Thank you Abba Father for totally healing me. No more Cancer - Ever!

This has been an amazing journey - road trip. I told a friend of mine last week that it has been delightful. He looked at me with a very strange look. It was a strange word wasn't it, Jesus, to come out of my mouth about Cancer after eight months?

But thinking about it this morning, Jesus... You laid the road ahead of me with rose petals as you are the Rose of Sharon. To be your sheep walking close to you with your hand on my head is delightful – "so delightful" are good words.

And I found Job 22:26: *"For then you will delight in the Almighty and lift your face to God."*

I want to stay close to you as we embark on another journey together. You lead and I will follow. I have learned these past eight months the depth of love you have for me and the trust I can have in you. If I just put one foot in the water then you will part the water. I am learning to have a gentle spirit that is pleasing to you."

Psalm 25:5: *"Lead me in Thy truth and teach me, for Thou art the God of my salvation."*

I am ready to learn new things. Lead on, Lord Jesus. I am going to end the book with the following... might as well end the journey with it as well.

"For I know the plans that I have for you, declares the LORD. Plans for welfare and not for calamity to give you a future and a hope." Jeremiah 29:11

Looking back over the year, I know the above is true. If it is true for me it is true for you, too!

Isaiah 49:11 says, *"Behold I have inscribed you on the palms of my hands; your walls are continually before me."*

Be Encouraged. As I re-read this the tears are flowing and all I can say is, "Thank you, Jesus. Thank you Jesus."

T.

CHAPTER 9 – MARCH

Outgoing Email: March

This journey is over. The last page of the book is being read and the cover is closing on it. Thank you all. I am crying as I write this... How to end? I can't. You all are so important to me... We have laughed, cried, prayer together in person, over the phone and through emails. Know I will continue to pray for you all, a habit when I walk Annie in the early morning as the sun is just breaking the horizon. I am thankful the Cancer journey is over.

"Trust in the LORD with all your heart and lean not on your own understanding; in all your ways acknowledge him, and he will direct your paths." (Proverbs 3, 5-6)

Goodbye for now...

Soli Deo Gloria (To God Be The Glory)

T.

ACKNOWLEDEMENTS

Quotes used in the book are used by permission from the following:

THE HUNGRY HEART: DAILY DEVOTIONS FROM THE OLD TESTAMENT by Jan Carlsberg, Hendrickson Publishing; Peabody, Mass. ISBN 1-56563-294-X.

OUR DAILY BREAD (For Personal and Family Devotions). RBC Ministries. 2012.

THE NEW AMERICAN STANDARD STUDY BIBLE. Copyright 1977 by The Lockman Foundation, La Habra, California. ISBN: 9781581351552.

MORNING AND EVENING: DAILY READINGS by Charles Haddon Spurgeon. Copyright 1995. Hendrickson Publishers, Inc.ISBN 978-1-56563-819-8.

LORD I WANT TO KNOW YOU by Kay Arthur. Copyright 1992 by Kay Arthur. Waterbrook Multnomah Publishing. ISBN: 1-57856.439.5.

MEETING GOD IN QUIET PLACES. Text Copyright 1992 by F. LaGard Smith. Published by Harvest House Publishers. Eugene, Oregon 97402.

SPRINGS IN THE VALLEY by Mrs. Charles E. Cowman. Zondervan Publishing. Grand Rapids, Michigan copyright 1939, 1968. This edition published in 1997. ISBN 0-310-21994-9.

STREAMS IN THE DESERT by Mrs. Charles E. Cowman. Zondervan Publishing. Grand Rapids, Michigan. Copyright 1925. Cowman Publication. Copyright renewal 1953, copyright 1965. Copyright 1996, Zondervan Corp. ISBN 10: 0-310-60705-1 and 13;978-0-310-60705-2.

JESUS CALLING - ENJOYING PEACE IN HIS PRESENCE by
Sarah Young. Copyright 2004 Thomas Nelson Publishing. Nashville,
TN. ISBN 13: 978-1-4041-1409-8.

To Contact the Author:

Email:

terrycwolfe@icloud.com

Made in the USA
Middletown, DE
01 July 2022

68018757R00106